THE

STUMP FARM

THE

STUMP FARM

Enjoy The memories

1997

ROBERT J. ADAMS

MEGAMY

THE PUBLISHER:
Megamy Publishing Ltd.
P. O. Box 3507
Spruce Grove, Alberta, Canada T7X 3A7

Canadian Cataloguing in Publication Data
Adams, Robert J., 1938-
   The stump farm

ISBN 0-9681916-1-4 (bound) -- ISBN 0-9681916-0-6 (pbk)

1. Farm Life--Alberta--Humor. 2. Canadian wit and humor (English)* I. Title.
PS8551.D3224S78 1997   C818'.5402   C97-910221-9
PR9199.3.A28S78 1997

Senior Editor: Kelly Hymanyk
Copy Editor: Linda Caldwell
Consulting Editor: Lola Gatzke
Design, Layout and Production: Kelly Hymanyk
Cover: Jason Bamford - Guideline Graphics
Printing: Quebecor Jasper Printing

DEDICATION

To my daughter Robin. Her ability to laugh in the face of adversity and persevere in spite of overwhelming personal hardship has been an inspiration to me and to the lives of those she has touched.

CONTENTS

ACKNOWLEDGEMENTS

I would like to thank my granddaughters Megan and Amy for allowing me to borrow their mommy for extended periods of time to assist me in working on this manuscript. Thanks to Bill my son-in-law for readily agreeing to babysit, giving Kelly the time necessary for this undertaking.

I can never thank my daughter Kelly enough for all the help she provided. It was Kelly who kept me on the straight and narrow, calling a spade a spade even when I thought it was a gem. It was Kelly's great editorial abilities that resulted in this book's completion.

Thanks to my wife Martha who had to suffer through the endless hours of obsessive behaviour I displayed since I commenced this project.

I must thank Don Milliken Sr. for kick-starting me. It was his words that blasted me from the comfort of retirement and prompted me to put pen to paper.

I would like to thank the following persons for their timely words of encouragement: Bob Cameron, Nancy Foulds, Barbara Smith.

A special thanks to my parents Bob and Florence Adams. The 1940's and early 50's were tough years in Western Canada. Jobs were scarce and money was even scarcer. They persevered and raised four children on farmland that at best would be described as marginal.

To my grandmother, Veona Ernst, the West's greatest cook. My Grandfather, John Ernst, to whom I will always be grateful, for without him, many of these stories would not have been lived.

INTRODUCTION

The early years of Robert Adams come to life in each of his stories. The setting, the characters and the situations are all based on personal experiences. He presents his stories as a knowing adult through the innocent eyes of a child. We must salute the author for his candid account of youth and his selfless sharing which allows us to love an irresistible little boy and his effortless enthusiasm.

Adams has the rare ability to laugh at himself as he becomes the unknowing victim in most of his stories. His natural ability to find enjoyment in these events, even years after they occur, attest to his strength of character to this day.

The recreation of an era long forgotten helps us appreciate the simplicity and hardships of a time that we will never see again; a time when laughter was important and one could laugh at himself while maintaining dignity.

MEGAMY PUBLISHING

THE

STUMP FARM

MY FRIENDS SURE ENJOYED FEEDING DOBBIN

"That's a real kid's horse alright, my boy rides him all the time. You can't go wrong with a horse like that," said the farmer admiring the horse.

"Well, your boy's quite a bit older than my Bob here," Dad replied and patted me on the shoulder. "I got to make sure the horse I get is nice and quiet."

I was feeling pretty important. I was with Dad and we were picking out a horse. Not just any horse. This was to be my horse. I was starting school in a few days, and I was getting my own saddle horse. I was going to have my very own horse and I would be riding him to school every day.

I had been the topic of discussion last night around the supper table. I was going to be six years old in October; it was time to go to school. We were living in a log house just off of Highway 16 near the Hornbeck turnoff. The closest school was at Marlboro, a Métis community, about three miles to the west. There were only two ways for me to get to that school, walk or ride a horse.

Mom was insistent that I was going to go to school, but she started to have second thoughts when Dad decided if that was the case, I needed a horse. "But Bob, he's so young," Mom had argued. "He's not old enough to handle a horse by himself."

"He's big enough and he's old enough," Dad responded. He was just as emphatic as Mom was. "He'll learn how to handle the horse. It'll make a man of him."

Now we were looking at horses with one of the few farmers in the country who had horses for sale.

"Like I was sayin', you don't have to worry none about this horse at all," said the farmer. "You take this horse and you got yourself a real bargain. Why that horse, he even knows the way to and from that school house better'n anybody. My boy rode him back and forth from that school house for the last few years now."

I stood there looking at the big horse waiting. He looked okay to me and I was itching to get in the saddle. Nobody spoke for awhile. Dad just walked around the horse and looked him over.

"Tell you what," said the farmer. "It's about the same distance from our place to yours as it is from your place to the school house. Why don't you put the saddle on him and let the boy ride him home? You can follow along behind in the truck. That should give you a good idea of how things will go. If you don't like him, bring him back. If you do, stop by anytime and pay me for him."

"That sounds like a fair deal to me," Dad responded. "Go grab the saddle, Bob, and we'll get you on the road."

I raced back to the truck. "I'm getting a horse!" I yelled at the rest of the family. "I'm going to name my horse Dobbin." I was so excited, I scampered onto the back of the truck and wrestled the saddle to the ground, then dragged it over to the horse.

"Are you sure you want to do this?" Mom asked Dad. "Look at him struggling with the saddle. He's not big enough. He can't even lift it. He can barely drag it. How's he going to manage when you're not around to help him?"

"Don't you worry your little head about that," Dad replied. "He'll be okay. I'll see to it."

"Well, I am worried about it," Mom snapped back. "He's my son and he's too young, I tell you."

Dad ignored her and saddled the horse, then lifted me into the saddle and handed me the reins. "Away you go," he said. "Just let him walk and he'll be okay. We'll be along in a few minutes."

Sitting atop the horse, the ground looked like it was a long way down. I grabbed onto the saddle horn and held on for dear life. "Giddyup," I said and the horse started to walk towards the road. As we walked past Mom, she managed a weak smile. She looked so sad. I, on the other hand, was anything but sad. I wanted everybody to see me. I was the cock of the walk, sitting astride my very own horse and praying that no one noticed I was white-knuckling the saddle horn. I forced a false smile.

Every day until school started, I was out at the barn with my horse, and every day Dad would come out and help me saddle him. Try as I might, I couldn't lift that saddle, let alone get it onto the horse. When the saddle was on him, I wasn't strong enough to snug up the cinch. I couldn't even get the bridle on him. But Dad was unconcerned. "Don't worry," he would say, "it's gonna be alright."

"Here's your lunch," Mom said as she handed me a cloth sack that contained my lunch for my first day in school. I was sitting in the saddle atop my horse just as proud as a peacock.

"We'll follow along behind and see how things go," Dad said. "If you boys are ready to go you can get in the truck," he directed the two teenage boys standing in the yard. One was the son of the farmer who sold us the horse, the other was his friend. They were both about fifteen. Dad had recruited them to help me with the horse before and after school.

Ordinarily they would walk to school, but because they were going to help me, Dad was giving them a ride. They were my new friends, and I liked them immediately.

Mom walked along beside Dobbin as he walked out of the yard and onto the highway. She kept looking up at me. Her eyes were really sad. I thought she was going to cry.

Dobbin walked down the highway, past the General Store on the north side of the highway and turned right, taking the road into Marlboro. The old cement smoke stack that stood like a silent sentinel looked monstrous as Dobbin and I walked beneath it.

Dobbin approached a broken-down old building and stopped. This wasn't the school house, I could see the school from there, but we weren't at it yet. I kicked him in the ribs, but he just stayed put. I kicked harder. The stupid horse wouldn't move.

"Hold on now," I heard Dad call out from the truck. "That's the barn. Dobbin will be staying in there while you're in school. You can climb on down now."

I swung my leg over the saddle horn and fell to the ground. The two teenagers came over and took Dobbin into the barn, unsaddled him and gave him some hay. "Don't worry about anything, Mr. Adams," said the farmer's son. "We'll look out for him."

Dobbin was safe in the barn with a manger full of hay

and I was strolling across the field with my new friends. It was my first day at school and I was the only one there with his own horse. I was pretty important.

At lunch time I hurried up and ate so that I could go to the barn and check on Dobbin. My friends told me that would be a good idea and they would come with me. It became our daily routine.

After school, my friends saddled Dobbin and helped me into the saddle. They were true friends. They walked alongside of Dobbin as we headed back to our place. Dad met us along the rode and gave my friends a ride. Back at our barn, they unsaddled Dobbin and said they would see me in the morning.

"How was the first day of school?" Mom asked when we were all sitting around the supper table.

"It was really good," I replied.

"How did you manage with the horse?" she asked with concern.

"Good," I replied. "My friends took care of him for me, they fed him and everything. They even came over to the barn with me at lunch and helped me feed Dobbin. They said they would help me every day. They're real good friends, I like them."

"I told you it would be okay," Dad addressed Mom. She cast a swift look in his direction.

"We'll see," Mom glared at Dad. "We'll just wait awhile and see how helpful they really are. This is just the first day. There's still lots of days left in this school year." Mom wasn't convinced.

By the end of the first week, everything was down to a routine. Dad had been right. There was no need to worry about me. My friends came around in the morning and saddled Dobbin. They walked to school with me and looked after Dobbin there. Then after school they brought me back home and unsaddled Dobbin.

It seemed to me that Mom's eyes were looking sadder every day as she watched me ride off to school.

After a month, Mom was getting more concerned then ever. She was really questioning my riding Dobbin to school and back every day. "Have you taken a good look at your son lately?" she asked Dad.

"He looks fine to me," he said, casting a glance in my direction.

"Take a better look," she snapped.

Dad took another look at me and I looked down to see if I was missing something.

"Just look at him," she said angrily. "He can hardly keep his eyes open. He's dead tired. Last night he fell asleep during supper. I tell you riding that horse is too much for him."

"He'll get used to it," Dad said. "It just takes a little time. It'll make a man out of him."

"But he's so young," she protested. "I just don't like to see him out on that highway every day on that horse. I've been thinking and I've changed my mind. I think we should wait another year before we send him to school."

"I tell you he's fine," Dad repeated. "We'll just give him a little more time. I'm sure he'll snap out of it."

The next day at school, when the lunch hour started, my friends came over to my desk.

"What say we have lunch at the barn with Dobbin again today?" said the farmer's son. "We need you, Bob," his friend chimed in. "You're an important part of our team, big guy." They both laughed.

"Oh boy, you bet," I replied.

Whenever my new friends wanted to have lunch at the

barn, that meant that they were taking a couple of girls along.

Five of us walked over to the barn at lunch to check on Dobbin and give him more hay and some oats. It was a routine that I had become familiar with since the first week of school.

"Okay Bob," they said to me when we got to the barn. "We'll go in and feed Dobbin. Like your Dad said, that's big guy's work. You stay out here in the fresh air and eat your lunch, okay? Now remember, you're our friend and friends have to look out for each other, right?"

"Right," I replied, happy that I could help my friends.

"Now, what are you going to do if you see someone coming?"

"I'm gonna knock on the door," I said seriously.

"Good man," they said and each patted me on the back as they followed the girls into the barn.

Checking on Dobbin and feeding him hay at lunch hour had been the brainchild of my new-found friends. Everyday, as regular as clock work, the three of us would walk over to the barn at lunch time. However, shortly after Dad had stopped monitoring our routine, two of the girls from school occasionally joined us on the daily check of Dobbin. They would accompany us, or rather my two friends, two or three times a week. "Remember, we'll call you in a little later and you can check to see that we fed Dobbin enough, okay? But you gotta wait until we call, right?" one of them would confide in me.

"Right," I replied and took up my post outside the door.

My friends sure enjoyed feeding Dobbin, especially when the girls helped. I could hear them laughing and giggling in there. I enjoyed feeding Dobbin too, but I never found that much to laugh about.

Just before the lunch hour ended, my friends and the girls would come out. I could tell that the girls had helped with the hay because they were always busy brushing it off each other and picking it out of their hair. Then I would get to go into the barn to check on Dobbin. His manger would be full of hay and he would have some oats. My friends really took care of my horse.

"You're the best kind of friend, Bob," they would tell me on the way back to the school house and pat me on the back. I always felt real proud. They were two of the biggest kids in school and they were my friends.

We left the school at the end of the day and just like any other day, they saddled Dobbin and brought him out of the barn, then hoisted me into the saddle. We all left the barn together, my friends walking, me riding Dobbin. I stayed in the saddle until we were out of sight of the school.

As soon as we rounded the corner, as usual my friends would get me out of the saddle and they would climb on. Away down the road Dobbin would gallop. Like clockwork, my friends would yell back at me. "C'mon Bob, we'll race you to the corner. You better hurry, you don't want your Dad to have to come looking for you, now do you?" and they would laugh. I didn't want to get into trouble with Dad, so I ran along behind as fast as I could go. I tried my best to keep up, but they were always way ahead of me.

My friends and Dobbin galloped off down the highway and were out of sight. I was running along the edge of the ditch, going past the General Store, when I heard someone call my name. I stopped and looked around. I heard it again.

"Bob. Come here, son."

It sounded like Dad. I looked over at the store and there he was standing in the doorway. Boy will my friends be happy to see Dad, I thought, as I walked over.

When I got to the store, Dad squatted down in front of me. He wasn't smiling and I knew I was in big trouble. "I saw your horse go by, son." He looked very serious. "How come you're not riding him?"

I kicked at the rocks on the driveway and looked down at my feet. I didn't want to tell on my friends, but then there was nothing to tell, Dad already knew what was happening.

"I dunno," I whispered, afraid that I might say the wrong thing.

"How long has this been going on?" he asked.

"I dunno, for a while, I guess."

"I guess?" he replied. "Did they tell you not to tell me?"

"Uh huh, I guess so."

"Tell you what, son, how about you go get yourself a soda pop. Then, you and I can go and surprise your friends." He smiled. "Think that would be fun?"

"Yeah," I said excitedly as I ran to grab a pop. "I'll bet they'll be real surprised to see you, Dad."

"I'll just bet they will." Dad didn't smile when he said that. He picked me up and carried me over to his truck. Dad wasn't in a hurry as he drove down the road towards my friends and home. He followed along behind them for quite a ways before one of them looked back and saw us.

Man, Dad was right. My friends were really surprised to see Dad following them.

Back in the truck, we could hear the farmer's son yell, "Whoa!" as he yanked back on Dobbin's reins. They were both in such a hurry to get off Dobbin that they fell out of the saddle and sprawled on the ground.

"You stay right here," Dad said to me as he got out of the truck. He walked over to my friends. They just stood there with their heads down looking at the ground and they weren't saying anything as he talked to them. Then I heard him say as he raised his voice something that sounded like, "...before I skin you alive!"

They turned around real smart like and started walking down the road leading Dobbin. Dad and I drove along behind in his truck.

"How come they're not riding Dobbin?" I asked Dad.

"I don't think they have any desire to ride right now," he replied.

"Should I ride Dobbin? Then they could ride with you."

"I don't think they want to ride with me either." He smiled at me. "Right now, I think they're quite happy to be able to walk." All the way home, they never looked around once.

Back at our place, my friends unsaddled Dobbin and then they left. The farmer's son was leading Dobbin out of the yard.

"Now don't you forget to tell your Dad what happened today and I'll be over tomorrow to talk to him," Dad hollered after them. Neither one turned around or acknowledged that they heard him.

That night at the supper table, I was the centre of attention again.

"I told you he was too young to be riding that horse down that highway," Mom said angrily.

"It wasn't him," Dad replied, not wanting to concede anything. "It was those other two. They took advantage of him."

"Well I told you to wait awhile and see how reliable they were, didn't I? I didn't like those two anyway. As far as I was concerned, they were just a couple of sneaks. No good if you ask me. I just wonder what else they took advantage of?" Mom asked, staring a hole right through me.

"They're my friends," I protested to Mom, defending them. "They trusted me whenever we went to the barn to feed Dobbin at lunch time."

"What do you mean they trusted you? Why shouldn't they? All you did was check on the horse, wasn't it?"

I looked down at my plate to avoid her eyes. She wanted me to tattle on my friends, I just knew it.

"Well, wasn't it?" she demanded.

I knew it, she wants me to be a snitch. "I can't tell. They're my friends, and you don't snitch on friends."

"You better tell your mother if there's something else that we should know about," Dad said, entering the conversation and taking Mom's side.

"There's nothing," I answered, fidgeting in my chair. "They said they'd beat me up if I told anybody."

"I don't think they'll be beating anybody up," Dad said quite calmly. "Tell your mother what she wants to know."

"Well, some days at noon when we'd go over to feed Dobbin, I'd have to stand guard at the door," I mumbled, knowing that I had broken my friends' trust.

"Why were you standing guard at the door, if they were just feeding the horse?" Mom asked, looking at Dad for an answer. He shrugged his shoulders.

"It was only on the days they had the girls with them," I said. "They stayed in there the whole lunch hour, laughing and giggling. I think they were smoking," I added quickly.

The silence that engulfed our kitchen table was deafening. It hung in the air for an eternity and then Mom turned and looked at Dad.

"Smoking indeed," Mom said and for the first time in a month, I saw a smile cross my mother's face. My naive

23

comment had driven home her point.

I never returned to the Marlboro school house that year, or any other year. The next summer we moved to a farm outside of Edson, where I started school in the fall with my sister Gwen.

And so began my memorable adventures on the Stump Farm.

NICK THE DOG MAN

One dog barked and suddenly there was a whole chorus of dogs barking, snarling and snapping. The trees were full of mad dogs. Each and every one of them sounded like they wanted a little piece of me.

"I'll bet there are thousands of them," I yelled to my sister, as the first of the dogs charged through the heavy trees. They were coming right at us. "Run for your life! They're after us!" I yelled. "They're gonna kill us!" We took off down the road just as fast as our little legs would carry us.

There were two old bachelors living on the south road, and we had to pass by both of their places going to and from town. They were as opposite as night and day. Nick the Dog Man surrounded himself with dogs and avoided people. Gutsky had not a single pet and his door was always open. He welcomed guests.

It was the first day of school for us and we were walking home for the first time since we had moved to Edson. We had just started to walk past Nick the Dog Man's place when the first dog barked. We knew enough to be very quiet when walking past Nick's, but with the excitement of school, we had much to talk about. Our exuberance had been heard by the pack and now we were running for our lives.

We never looked back, but we knew there were hundreds of dogs barking, snarling and snapping at our heels. At any moment they would overtake us and tear us to pieces.

Well, they were barking and snarling, and surely would have been snapping at our heels if they could have. The fact that most were chained to kennels or trees never entered our minds.

Past Nick the Dog Man's place we sped. Past the old bachelor Gutsky's place we literally flew.

Once we crossed the driveway and were in the safety of our yard, we started yelling at the top of our lungs. "Help. Help. Help. Nick's dogs are after us!" we wailed. "They're trying to kill us! They're going to tear us to pieces. Help, Mom, help!"

Mother came flying out of the house at the sound of us howling like we were being torn limb from limb. "What's the matter? What's all this noise about? Quiet now. Quiet. Slow down and tell me what all this fuss is about."

"Nick's dogs chased us all the way home," we wailed. "They tried to bite us and kill us. We're never going to school again if we have to walk by Nick the Dog Man's place."

"Hush now, hush. I don't see any dogs," she said calmly. "Where are they?"

I turned around and looked back towards the gate. Sure enough, Mom was right. There were no dogs. There was nothing but the gate, the road and lots of trees.

"They chased us right to the gate and were trying to bite

us. There were thousands of them," we offered. Our imaginations had been jump-started and we were not about to back off just because there were no dogs in sight.

In the distance, the chorus from many dogs could still be heard. We walked with mother back to the gate and looked down the road in the direction of Nick the Dog Man's place. There was not a sign of any dog on the road. But they had been there, thousands of them.

Nick the Dog Man was an old bachelor who lived about a quarter of a mile from our place and he raised dogs. The truth of the matter is that he raised hundreds of dogs. He had dogs of all breeds and sizes, but mostly he had mongrels.

Nick's place was set back from the road in the trees. The heavy growth of pine and spruce trees along the road made it impossible to see into his yard. From the road, one would never suspect there was a house in there let alone the massive collection of canines that awaited the unsuspecting. If the dogs didn't bark, a person could walk right past his place and not know there was anything there.

Most of Nick's dogs were tied to dog houses that were scattered all over his property, but the puppies were left to run at will. Sometimes those puppies got to be pretty near full grown before Nick would chain them up.

It was these dogs, the puppies, that one often saw, because they responded to the slightest noise and charged towards the road. It only took one of Nick's dogs to bark to set off a ruckus that could be heard for miles. To a child walking by, it was a terrifying experience. It was an experience that I would dread every school day for six years.

"You've got to do something about those dogs. The children are terrified of them," I heard my mother tell Dad. "I want you to go down there and tell Nick to keep those dogs chained up. The kids will be walking by there every day coming from school and I don't want another scene like I had today."

"Okay, I'll see what I can do," Dad said and left the house.

We all raced to the road, and watched in terror as Dad walked down the road and turned towards Nick's place. The instant he walked through the trees, those dogs began to bark and snarl. They meant business. We were sure that Dad would never return, that he would be torn to pieces and eaten by Nick's dogs.

As we waited by the road, the barking slowly subsided. Then there was only silence, deathly silence as we waited and watched.

"There's Dad!" someone shouted as a figure emerged from the trees and walked to the road. We all cheered. Dad had survived. He had faced Nick the Dog Man and his vicious dogs and he had survived.

"There's no problem," Dad proclaimed. "Nick has all his dogs chained to dog houses. I think maybe you kids let your imaginations run wild this afternoon. There's the odd puppy running loose, but that's nothing to be scared of. You're not afraid of puppies, are you?" he asked.

We all shook our heads. We weren't afraid of puppies.

"Good. Now I don't want you to worry none, those puppies won't hurt you. They probably won't even leave the yard. They just bark a lot."

Despite Dad's assurances, those dogs still scared the living tar out of us. Each night after school, we would try to sneak past Nick the Dog Man's place. However, one little sound and those dogs would commence to bark and howl. Several hundred dogs barking at the same time can be very intimidating.

Every time the dogs barked, those puppies that were running loose would come racing through the trees towards the road and panic would set in. Man, but some of those puppies were big hummers and whenever they appeared we would find ourselves fleeing for our lives. We would race down the road and into our yard yelling and screaming bloody murder. Mother would come flying out of the house to check on the extent of the damage and offer comforting words. "Wait until Dad gets home, he'll take care of everything."

Every night that the dogs barked and we ran, Mom would be waiting for Dad to get home. She would have a few words with him about the dogs and away he would go once more to Nick the Dog Man's place.

Sunday evenings were normally quiet on the south road. It was because of the lack of foot traffic on this evening that Nick's dogs would not be barking their fool heads off at some unseen traveller.

At six o'clock every Sunday evening—you could set your clocks by it—Gutsky would entertain us with the melodic sounds of his flute. The pure clear notes would float through the quiet Sunday evenings. It was a time for one to stop and reflect on the activities of the week.

It was six o'clock on Sunday evening and we were playing on the road near our driveway waiting for Dad. He had been away on a job and was expected to be home this evening. The air was full of the sound of Gutsky's flute when we spotted Dad walking down the road. He was on shanks ponies, the most common mode of transportation available at the time.

The sight of Dad prompted us all to wave and call greetings long before he could hear our voices. He waved back and that prompted more waving and more shouting.

Our calls did not go unanswered.

However, it was Nick's dogs who commenced barking and howling in reply. We could see several of the puppies emerge from the trees and gather on the road; they too were waiting for Dad. However, they didn't concern Dad one little bit. I watched with pride. Not once did he break stride as he walked up to those puppies and continued on past. Just like he had told us to do, he paid them no heed. He just kept walking towards us and we ran to meet him.

There were puppies all around him. They were barking, yipping and jumping. The puppies were also happy to see Dad. Suddenly one of them came up from behind and nailed him, nipped him right on the cheek of his arse.

Now my Dad was known for his quiet manner. He was calm, easy-going, had the patience of Job and was never seen to rush. But that nip unleashed some pent-up energy and fury foreign to our eyes. It caused us all to freeze in our tracks.

Dad suddenly sprang into the air and let out a bellow that could be heard clear back into town. When he came down on the road, he aimed a boot at the closest pup. The pups scattered and Dad sprinted for the side of the road.

"Look at Dad!" I yelled. "Wow, is he ever fast!"

He leapt over the ditch that was full of water. His legs stretched out like a long jumper, one giant step and he literally flew over the fence like a hurdler.

"Holy cow! Did you see Dad jump the ditch and the fence?"

Dad disappeared into the bush on the far side of the road. The puppies stayed on the road barking after their retreating prey. With the puppies on the road, we started backing towards our own driveway and safety.

"There's Dad!" someone shouted.

I turned around and sure enough Dad was climbing over the fence. He was coming back to the road. He wasn't moving quite as fast coming back out as he had been going in. In his hands he was clutching a hunk of deadfall about the size of a baseball bat. The puppies were all standing at the edge of the road barking their greetings, welcoming him back. He jumped the ditch and landed on the edge of the road, right among the puppies. They rushed in and he swung his club like he was Babe Ruth, swinging for the fence. Suddenly puppies were flying in every direction. With every swing another pup would let out a yelp and limp for home.

Dad and his club followed them, across the road, onto the driveway and disappeared into the trees leading to Nick the Dog Man's place. He was in there for a long time before he finally walked back out to the road and turned towards home.

"I don't think that you'll have to worry about any of those dogs again," he said as Mom was busy putting mercurochrome on the gash on his butt. "Nick promised that from now on, all the dogs would be tied, even the puppies."

For many people, just hearing the William Tell Overture conjures up the sight of the Lone Ranger with his trusty sidekick, Tonto, as they gallop across the open plains. For me, the sound of Gutsky's flute at six o'clock on a Sunday evening would forever revive the vivid memory of my father gracefully sailing over the ditch and clearing the fence in one fluid motion.

THE MUDDY ROAD

"Oh my good Lord, Bobby, just look at you. You're covered in mud." My mother sounded utterly horrified as she turned and looked at me standing in the doorway. "What happened to you? Are you hurt?"

I was seven years old and had just arrived home from school. Like every other day during my first year of school, I had walked the two miles, all the way from Edson to our farm on the south road. It was spring break-up. The snow was almost all melted. The ditches were full of water and the road was a sea of mud. On this day I had skilfully negotiated my way past Nick the Dog Man's place without disturbing his dogs.

Before I could answer, she noticed that I wasn't wearing my rubber boots.

"And where are your boots? What did you do with them?" She didn't sound horrified now. Now she sounded slightly peeved, in fact, it sounded very much like "you need a good swat on the butt" tone of voice.

"Oh, I'm okay," I gave her a big old reassuring grin

32

while my teeth chattered uncontrollably. I was shaking so hard I was sure she could hear my knees knocking. "But I lost my boots coming home."

"Now how could you possibly lose your boots?" she asked.

"I lost them in the road," I offered and attempted to hide my muddy feet behind my sopping wet muddy trousers. Bad move on my part. Now Mom noticed that I didn't have any socks on, either.

"You don't have any socks on, and just what have you done with them?" she yelled as if suddenly wracked with great pain.

"I lost them, too," I answered in a whisper. I didn't like the look in Mom's eyes. I think she was getting quite irritated now.

"How could anyone possibly lose their boots and socks walking home from school?" she fumed.

"They just got stuck in the mud when I was walking down the road and I couldn't get them out," I answered almost apologetically. "I tried, Mom, honest I did, but they were really stuck tight. Honest."

Mom didn't often get angry with one of us kids, but I could tell that she was not pleased with me at that moment.

We had moved to the farm the previous summer. This was our first spring on the south road and our first real taste of the muddy roads that would come with spring break-up. The south road was a dirt road composed entirely of clay, the gooey sticky kind. There was no rock or gravel to mar its surface. During spring break-up, the entire length of the road was a sea of mud with a mind of its own.

The south road, as we called it, grudgingly, and I mean very grudgingly, allowed passage in the springtime. On this spring day, the south road was at its worst and I was its victim. Clay is not the best surface for driving or walking on when it's damp, but when it's wet, as it was on this day, it is just about impossible for man or beast or car to traverse.

Except for one small detour around a small creek, the south road ran straight south from the CNR tracks southeast of Edson. There were less than a dozen farms along the south road and each had its own driveway. Each driveway had been built over a culvert, which was a long wooden box about twelve inches square, running its entire length. These culverts were laid lengthways at the bottom of the ditch and then covered with earth, more clay. This allowed for free passage of water as it drained along the ditches. These wooden culverts worked well for a couple of years and then they would either plug up or the boards would rot from being in the wet clay and they would collapse.

Most of the culverts on the south road had collapsed. In the spring when the snow melted, as it had been doing for the past few weeks, it did not drain. The water stayed in the ditches where it was trapped by the solid driveways that served as dams at every farm.

When the ditches got full, they would overflow and the water would cover the road. Water on the road would fill the ruts and wherever there was a depression, a small lake would form. Most of the drainage flowed north, through the ruts towards the detour, the gully and the small creek. In the gully there was always a small lake where the road crossed the stream. The little stream was hard-pressed to carry all the runoff water pouring into it. In the spring time, the ditches were always full of water and the road was always muddy and dotted with small lakes.

During the muddy season, the first car that travelled

down the road would make a set of ruts. Each passing vehicle would add to the depth of the ruts until they were axle deep. That would have been about knee deep on me.

On this day, the ditches on both sides of the road were full with muddy water. It was through the ruts that the water was finding the least obstructed path to the small stream north of our farm and leaving little lakes covering the low spots.

It was along this wet, muddy, rutted, clay-based south road, the source of all my problems, that I had just walked home from school. Mother was literally hovering over me now, waiting for an answer.

"They're back on the road," I replied.

"You get yourself out of those wet duds before you catch your death of cold, and then you just skeedaddle your butt back there and pick them up before I paddle your backside. Do you understand me?"

That I understood real well. "I can't," I stammered.

"Don't you give me that 'I can't,' young man. You get right back out there and get them boots, right now. I won't tell you again. Now hurry up and get changed."

"I can't," I wailed. "They're stuck in the mud."

"What do you mean they're stuck in the mud?"

"They're stuck in the mud in the road."

After crossing the railroad tracks, I had turned onto the south road staying to one side where the walking was pretty good. Off the road itself there was lots of dead grass and brush, but there was no mud. When I got to the gully I had to go on to the road to cross the bridge over the small creek. Right then it was not a small creek, it was a big creek or a small lake with all the water rushing into it. I had to be careful wading through the water that was covering the bridge because it was close to the tops of my rubber boots and I didn't want to get wet.

After passing through the gully I didn't go back to the side of the road where the walking was good, instead I stayed on the clay road and slogged my way homeward through the mud. I soon discovered that if I walked in the ruts, walking was much easier, because the bottom of the rut was packed quite hard. It was a little slippery so I had to be careful not to lose my balance.

Outside the ruts walking was a little more difficult as my feet would not only sink into the mud, they would grow with each step as the clay built up around the sides of my boots. The depth I would sink in the mud depended on the amount of water. The more water on the surface, the deeper my foot would submerge. The less water, the more the clay would stick. But I was having fun and making good time getting home via the rut route. Boy those ruts were the ideal place to walk. I couldn't wait to tell everyone about my discovery.

I hadn't gone far when I came to a little dip in the road. Here the flow of water was impeded and a small lake had formed, filling the ditches and spreading into the bush on both sides of the road. No problem for me, I could walk through this with my eyes shut, I'd just follow the ruts where the walking was good. I could see where the ruts were by the lines of mud that had been pushed up by the tires. I waded in.

I had taken only a few steps into the lake when suddenly the bottom fell out of the rut. First one foot got wet, then the other. Wow, that muddy water was sure cold. Pretty soon I was in water over my knees, but I was a trooper and not afraid of a little water, so I waded on. I could see the other side. But the water was cold and I started to shiver. Maybe I should get out of the rut and walk on the road, I thought. The water won't be as deep, I reasoned. I stepped out of the rut and into the mud.

I was right, it wasn't nearly as deep. With my first step I felt the mud about four inches under the surface of the water. As I put my weight down, my foot started to sink into the mud and continued until there was about a 1/2 inch of my rubber boot showing above the water. I lifted my other foot out and stepped down, down to the same depth. Then I tried to lift my first foot. It was stuck. Not being able to lift the first foot had not really occurred to me and my speedy mind had already set the second foot in motion. It too was stuck.

My body had been anticipating that my feet would move and I was suddenly having a tough time staying upright. I flailed my arms around wildly trying to regain my balance. First forward, then backward, then forward again. But my boots remained firmly planted, stuck in the mud. Gravity overcame me and I sat down right beside the ridges, right beside the rut, right in about four inches of muddy water and sticky clay. Wow, now I was really wet and muddy. I knew Mom was going to be mad.

The only way I could stand up was to get out of my rubber boots, but that was not easy since they were stuck tight in the mud. I rolled around and thrashed about wildly trying to get those boots off and succeeded in getting covered with mud and water before freeing my feet. I was chilled to the bone when I finally got up, without my boots on. I tried to pull them out of the mud. No luck. I tried everything I could, but that mud would not let go. Those little black tops were just visible above the water, and that is where they would stay.

Now, I knew I was in deep trouble. And with a heavy heart and a sinking feeling, I headed home. I tried the muddy road, but it was too tough to walk on with socking feet, so I dropped back into the water filled ruts. Somewhere between the boots and our driveway, I walked out of my socks. I felt like an icicle when I showed up in our doorway barefoot, soaking wet and covered in mud.

"You wash yourself off now and I'll go back with you. Now hurry up before it gets dark."

"What am I going to wear? I don't have any boots now," I complained.

"You'll have to wear your shoes."

"But they'll get all muddy," I protested.

"Don't argue with me. Now you get moving before I lose my temper."

I got out of my cold dirty clothes and put some warm water in the basin and washed up. Mom got me some clean clothes and my good oxfords. I put them on and followed her out the door.

"What happened to your socks?" Mom asked again as we headed up the road. This time I walked on the side of the road with Mom. She didn't think much of my idea of walking in the ruts.

"I lost them, too. I think they're in the ruts," I replied.

"Where in the ruts?"

"I don't know, I don't even remember them coming off."

"I don't believe this," Mom said.

We made a mistake and we knew it instantly. We were both so concerned about my boots that we were talking as we walked past Nick the Dog Man's place. Suddenly there was a chorus of yelps and barks and about a dozen dogs, mostly pups, rushed out to the road to growl and bark at us. I was almost glad to see those pups come out, because Mom's attention was now focused totally on them. She forgot about me for a minute or two and watched those dogs suspiciously. Mom didn't like them anymore than I did.

Mom looked at the dogs charging through the trees. "Well, old Nick certainly hasn't tied those dogs up, has he," she stated.

"You have to be real quiet when you walk past Nick the Dog Man's place," I said to Mom.

She wasn't impressed with my knowledge. I could tell by the look I got.

"Dad said not to worry about them. They're only pups and won't hurt you if you showed them you weren't afraid," I offered again. That comment brought a real mean look. Then I remembered Dad getting nailed in the butt and I didn't offer any more words of wisdom.

"Do you know where you left your boots?" Mom quizzed me when we were past the dogs.

"I think so, they're down more towards the top of the gully. I didn't leave them, Mom. They're stuck in the mud, honest," I protested.

We walked about another quarter of a mile.

"Right there," I said, pointing to the centre of the small lake that ran from ditch to ditch and stretched for a couple hundred yards along the length of the road. We were standing on the side of the road across the ditch and I could just see two little black rings above the surface of the water. "See them? They're right over there by the ruts. You can just see the tops of them sticking out of the water."

Everywhere I looked there was water, in both ditches and on the road. The only mud visible was the little ridges that identified the path of the ruts. The ridges of mud looked just like little mountains sticking out of the ocean, and just on the far side of the ruts, my rubber boots were beckoning. The tops of my boots looked a long way out from where we were standing. Mom stood and looked at the sea of water with the little ridges forming four straight lines. I could tell that she could see my rubber boots, too, and she was not pleased with me.

"What were you doing out there?" Mom asked helplessly.

"Walking home."

"But why in the middle of the road in all that mud and water?"

"It was easier to walk in the ruts. The ground is harder there," I answered, quite pleased with the information I had gained earlier in the day.

"My boots didn't get stuck until I got out of the ruts and into the mud. Then I couldn't pull them out. I tried to, but then I fell. When I got my feet free, I tried to pull them out with my hands, but they still wouldn't come out."

"Where did you lose your socks? Are they still in your boots?"

"No. They were on when I started walking, but they came off in the ruts. I don't know where."

Mom just kept staring at that water and shaking her head.

"I can't cross the ditch here," she said, "it's full of water."

"Do you want me to go and get them? I'm not afraid of the water."

"I think that you've done quite enough for one day. You stay right here. I'll go down to a driveway and come back on the road."

"Don't forget to walk in the ruts, Mom," I offered, quite proud of the fact that I knew where to walk. "It's a lot easier than trying to walk in the mud."

Mom walked a couple of hundred yards to a driveway and carefully, very carefully, stepped out onto the road. Her feet were growing with each step as the clay grabbed her boots and held on. When she reached the middle of the road, she turned and came walking towards me, right in the ruts like I told her to. I was very happy that I had been able to help her. When she neared the area where I was standing, she also reached the small lake covering the entire road. Very gingerly Mom started to wade in. She was moving much slower than I would have been. Cautiously she took one step and then looked around hoping that there was another way. There wasn't and she took a second and a third step.

"Stay in the ruts, Mom," I yelled very knowledgeably, "or you'll get stuck in the mud."

Mom paused quite often and gave me a glare. She wasn't at all pleased with me. She stayed in the ruts as long as she could, but the water was getting mighty close to coming over the top of her boots. She was walking awfully slow, taking real small steps. As she entered deeper water I noticed that Mom had to lift her feet higher because the ruts were too narrow for her to move one foot past the other. Strange, I thought, I hadn't noticed that she was lifting her feet so high before. She sure looked funny, I chuckled to myself.

She stopped and looked at my boots. They were still quite a ways from her and she had gone as far as she could go without the water going over the tops of her boots. Mom looked over at me and I'm sure she would have gladly throttled me right then. She looked back at my boots and stepped out of the rut and into the mud. Instantly Mom found out what I already knew. Once that mud got hold of your boots it was not about to let them go. Mom was stuck.

"I'll help you," I yelled to her.

"You stay where you are!" she ordered as she tilted first one way, then the other. Suddenly, her arms were flailing wildly in the air as she fought gamely to keep her balance. Her body twisted and turned as she struggled to remain upright. One hand almost hit the water as she started to fall forward. She regained her balance, then almost fell over backwards. Mom wasn't going down without a fight. Boy, Mom sure looked funny, I thought, and I started to laugh. I knew Mom didn't think it was funny as gravity overcame her best efforts and she tilted precariously to one side. One arm thrust out to help her steady herself, to break her fall. First her hand, then her arm disappeared into the water and mud. With a loud splash amid wild thrashing, Mom plowed sideways into the goop we called the south road.

"Are you okay, Mom?" I yelled again. "I'll come and help you."

"I told you to stay where you are, young man, and I mean it," she said as she struggled to pull herself up. Now I felt sorry for Mom seeing her thrashing around in the mud. There was no humour in her being in the same situation that I was earlier in the day.

When Mom had freed herself from her boots and was again standing she tried gamely to pull her boots out of the mud.

"They sure do get stuck in there, don't they?" I called out.

I got a cold glare and decided maybe I shouldn't say anymore. Mom's boots suffered the same fate as mine. Try as she might, she couldn't get them free.

Then she waded through the knee deep mud and water in her bare feet over to where my boots were still showing their little tops, like little black rings floating on the surface.

She grabbed first one then the other and tugged and pulled at them, but for all her strength and obvious fury, freedom for those boots was not to be.

"That mud is sure sticky, isn't it, Mom?"

"Yes, it is. And I don't want you walking in those ruts or down that road again. You stay off the road and walk on the side until it dries. Do I make myself clear?"

"Uh huh. I guess so," I answered.

Mom and I were walking home and she was holding my hand. I was feeling a little more secure now, because she didn't hold my hand on the way down the road to get my boots.

"Doesn't it feel funny when the mud squishes between your toes?" I asked as we walked home.

"Yes, it does," she replied, looking down at her naked feet.

MY BOY ALWAYS WINS

"Okay boy, you can take him. Here boy, let me fan you," he said, whipping off his shirt and flapping it up and down in front of my face. "Have a little sip of water. Here boy, loosen up your arms." He grabbed my wrists and shook my arms vigorously. "Shake them out real good, that's it. Now dance around a little," Grandfather yelled in my face.

Grandfather made sure that everyone standing around could hear him. With a big grin on his face, he winked at me. "Let's go and get him. You can take him with your eyes closed. You're my boy and my boys are always the best." He stepped around to my side and kept rubbing my shoulders and offering verbal encouragement.

"Don't worry, Grandfather, I can take him," I replied as I bounced around. I was as confident as Grandfather.

"Good boy. Just go right at him and don't stop. Don't give him a chance. He won't know what hit him. You're my boy and my boy always wins."

With those encouraging words from Grandfather, the

long wait was over. I had received boxing gloves for Christmas that year and ever since had been waiting for the weather to warm up.

"As soon as the weather is good we'll have boxing matches every Saturday morning," Mom had promised. This was the first Saturday that the weather was nice. The snow had melted and the ground was dry. Some of my cousins were at our farm to participate or watch. It was a family gathering. I was pretty important. I let everyone know as I strutted my stuff.

This Saturday morning of boxing was to be the first of many, I hoped. I had been waiting impatiently for this day. Now, after several months of wearing my boxing gloves in the house and swinging at imaginary opponents, I was ready for the real thing.

My first match was against my cousin. We were real close in age and I just knew I'd knock his block off. He didn't have a ghost of a chance. After all, I had been wearing the gloves all winter and practising. They were my gloves and I had tried on both sets often enough to know which ones were the best and I had the best ones on. My cousin had to settle for second best. If that wasn't enough, I had Grandfather in my corner.

I looked over at my cousin's corner and his trainer was standing beside him, his hands by his sides. They were both just standing there looking at me and Grandfather. His trainer wasn't saying anything. He wasn't giving him any tips or telling him what to do. They just stood there like statues. This was going to be easy, I smiled to myself.

It was then that I realized the value of a good trainer. Grandfather was getting me ready, loosening me up and giving me good tips. He was bouncing around, yelling and telling the world that his fighter could whip anybody.

Everyone's eyes were on Grandfather, watching him get his fighter primed. I could see the smiles on their faces as they nodded their approval of Grandfather's antics. Nope, my cousin wasn't being properly trained, I could see that and he'd pay for it. I was trained. I was primed. I was ready to go. Let the fight begin.

"Okay boys," said the referee, as he motioned to both corners. "Come on out here and get your instructions."

We both walked to the centre of the ring, which was actually just the rest of the family standing around in a circle. Our trainers came with us. Grandfather never quit talking. He sure could make a lot of noise. I'm not even sure what the instructions were, I never really heard them because Grandfather was yelling in my ear the whole time.

After the instructions, the referee said, "Back to your corners boys and come out fighting at the bell." We both walked back to our corners with our trainers. Grandfather was talking nonstop. He was more excited than I was and I was pumped.

The bell was an old cow bell and when it sounded, I charged out of my corner across the ring right at my cousin. I noticed his eyes darting from me to Grandfather and back again. He looked like a caged animal searching in vain for a place to hide. As I crossed the ring, Grandfather stayed right by my side, roaring in my ear. "Swing boy, swing. Hit him first. Don't give him a chance to hit you. Keep your guard up. That's it, boy, hit him again."

I was flailing away wildly. Half the time I think my eyes were closed, but then Grandfather had said I could beat him with my eyes closed. Finally, I connected. Somehow I had managed to hit him right in the eye. "Yeow, Owww oww," wailed my cousin as he covered his face with his gloved hands.

"Don't stop," yelled Grandfather. He was still by my side in the middle of the ring and screaming in my ear. "Hit him again, you got him now. Don't give him a chance, boy." My cousin was easy to hit now, because he was standing in the middle of the ring bawling his eyes out with his hands in front of his face. This was going to be a piece of cake. I didn't even have to close my eyes anymore because there was no fear now of getting hit. I lined him up to give him a good one, but the referee grabbed my hand. "That's it, Bobby," he said. "Fight's over. You're the winner," and he raised my hand.

Boy, I jumped up and down. Grandfather gave me a great big bear hug. Then I strutted around the ring like a peacock. Yep, I was the best and I didn't mind showing off either. But best of all I collected the winner's prize of 25 cents. Man, was I rich. I knew exactly what I was going to do with that 25 cents.

On Monday when I went to school, I flashed around my quarter to all my classmates. "Whipped my cousin in a boxing match," I boasted. "I'm going to go down to the CNR station and have lunch at the Beanery today," I tooted to all who were listening. Yup, for 25 cents I could get a hamburger, a bowl of soup and a coke. I was a big shot.

"We have boxing matches at our place every Saturday morning and I get to box my cousin," I warbled. The winner always gets 25 cents. "I'll probably have lunch at the Beanery every Monday," I crowed. There's no doubt about it, I was the cock of the walk.

Man, did I think I was something, sitting in the Beanery with all the railroaders. I sat on a stool at the counter and told the story to everyone. "You'll probably see me in here every Monday from now on," I boasted to the waitress.

Yessiree, for 25 cents I was going to be a regular. I could hardly wait for Saturday to roll around.

Finally, Saturday morning arrived and once again we were all gathered in our front yard for the weekly boxing matches. I was about to launch my defence and collect another quarter. I strutted around the yard like a Bantam Rooster. I wanted everyone to notice me before I took to the ring.

"Okay boy, you can take him. Let me fan you, boy," he said, stripping off his shirt. "Just go out there swinging and don't stop. Here boy, loosen up them arms. Now dance around a bit. That's it. Loosen up boy, loosen up, you're going to win. Remember, my boy always wins," roared Grandfather.

I stood there watching and listening to Grandfather going through the routine that I was pretty familiar with. Man, he never stopped moving or kept quiet. He was getting his fighter ready, and his fighter would be ready, I thought, as the lump in my throat grew and I started to have difficulty breathing.

On this Saturday morning, Grandfather was bouncing around in the opposite corner training my cousin. I had been abandoned. Now I got to stand there with my hands hanging loosely at my sides while my trainer stood idly by and watched Grandfather perform. I remembered last week when Grandfather was in my corner and I beat the tar out of my cousin. But now, watching Grandfather perform, I started to have doubts. What if I wasn't as good as I thought I was? Maybe I won just because Grandfather knew what he was doing and could get a fighter ready for the big one. Yeah, that was it, the key to winning was Grandfather. Now he was in the other corner and he was getting my cousin ready.

This time I was standing in the opposite corner and I mean standing. My trainer didn't know what he was doing. In fact he wasn't doing anything. He wasn't moving. He wasn't talking. He was just standing. We both just stood there watching Grandfather get his fighter ready.

I don't even remember who was in my corner. But it didn't matter who it was, I was quickly coming to the conclusion that Grandfather's corner would win because he knew what he was doing. He would jump around and yell a lot. He would give his fighter water. He would get him to dance around. He would shake his arms to loosen his muscles.

His opponent, me, just had to stand there with his statue of a trainer and wait for the inevitable. We hadn't even gone to the middle of the ring for instructions, let alone thrown a punch, and I was beat. My cousin would just close his eyes and whip me. Now, I wasn't even sure that I had the right gloves on. I couldn't tell by looking at them, but they didn't feel right. The fight hadn't started and already I hated this Saturday morning.

The referee called us to the centre of the ring. This time I heard everything he said. It would probably be the last thing I heard, I thought. I watched Grandfather and my cousin come across the ring. Grandfather never shut up and I started to think that he was awfully noisy. He was shouting into my cousin's ear all the time.

The cow bell rang and I took a step forward and stopped, just like my cousin had the week before. I watched as both he and Grandfather came bouncing across the ring at me. I looked first at my cousin. His eyes were wide open, his teeth were gritted; he was determined to rearrange my face. I looked at Grandfather and he was right beside my cousin coming across the ring. It looked like his nose was almost in my cousin's ear. No wonder he sounded so loud last Saturday. I looked back at my cousin. He was closing in fast flailing away like a windmill.

I ducked and heard a whiz go by my head as a haymaker missed. I may have blinked briefly or even closed my eyes, when suddenly there was this terrible splat as a boxing glove hit my nose. Instantly my eyes misted and everything sort of went black. I shook my head and took a quick peek. All I could see was brown boxing gloves whizzing around in front me like a swarm of bees. My cousin's face was right in front of me as he continued to flail away. He had murder in his eyes. It was payback time. I was wishing that the ground would open up and swallow me when I sort of felt and heard a sproing as another blow connected on the side of my head. Right on cue. "Yeow, Owwww oww," I wailed and threw my hands over my head to cover up as the referee stepped in and stopped the fight.

Now, it was my cousin's turn to bounce around the ring. I could only watch as he collected his quarter and strutted for the relatives.

We were supposed to box three rounds, but the bout never lasted that long. Grandfather's fighter would come bouncing out with all the confidence in the world that he had been prepared better than anyone else. His opponent would walk out and just stand there waiting to be destroyed. Neither boxer was disappointed. The inevitable would happen. The winner would get a quarter and the loser would pray for Grandfather in his corner the next week.

I was not hurt, although, like my cousin the week before, I wailed like I had been half-killed. But the worst hurt of all was watching my cousin collect the 25 cents.

What was I going to tell my classmates on Monday?

There would be no boasting. No Beanery. I wished I had just kept my mouth shut last week. Now it was not only my lunch I would have to eat in the classroom.

LISTEN, I HEAR ANOTHER SPEEDER

I was rushing to feed the chickens, because Dad had promised to take me grouse hunting as soon as my chores were finished, when I heard the noise. Wop...wop...wop...wop...wop...wop...wopwop whirrrrr.

"There," I said to my brother, who was helping me, "I heard it again. Did you hear it?"

"Yeah, I heard it, too. What was it?"

"It's a speeder. I've heard it several times and it's just back of the barn."

"Let's go and see if we can find it."

"We can try, but we won't find it. I've looked all over back there, and there's no railroad tracks anywhere," I replied. "At least I can't find them if there are."

Forgetting about the chickens and the grouse hunt for the moment, we walked out behind the barn to a stand of spruce and pine to begin our search for the speeder.

We both knew what a speeder sounded like and what a speeder looked like. Every day that we went to school, we had to cross the CNR tracks north of us. Sometimes we would even walk home through the railway switch yards that had hundreds of boxcars, locomotives and 'speeders'.

'Speeders' were small flat-topped motorized vehicles. They had four steel wheels and ran on the railway tracks, just like all the other railroad engines. The section crews always used 'speeders' and the pop...pop...pop...pop...pop of their motors was always heard around the tracks.

Sometimes in the dead of winter when the weather was extremely cold and there was no wind, the sounds from the switch yards could be clearly heard, like they were right there in our yard. Other than that, we never heard any of the train noises, except in the spring. Then we would hear the 'speeders' everywhere. It was the strangest thing. This one sounded like it was right behind the barn.

We searched all over in the trees back of the barn, but no luck. We couldn't find the tracks, let alone the speeder. So we walked back to the house, still mystified. It sounded like that speeder was right there and yet it wasn't.

We had no sooner returned to the yard when wop...wop...wop...wop...wop...wop...wopwop whirrrrr, there it was again. We looked at each other in amazement, it was the darndest thing.

Guns played an important role in the life of a farm boy in western Alberta, and they were certainly very important to me. Mom said I wasn't old enough to handle a gun yet, but Dad said I was getting close and would soon be able to hunt with a .22 calibre rifle. We didn't have one in our house, but I sure longed for the day when I could get one.

Being allowed to accompany Dad when he went hunting was a thrill beyond belief. Our hunting trips were only day outings, but they may just as well have lasted a week for all of the adventure they provided.

On this day, a fine spring day, Dad was hunting for Ruffed Grouse. He cautioned us that we were not to discuss our hunting trips with anybody. He would never come home empty-handed and it pained me to no end not to be able to boast to my friends at school.

There was never a thought, certainly not on my part, of having to hunt in any particular season. As I often heard, "A man hunts when he needs something for the table," and so it was with my family. Spring days were always good days for hunting Ruffed Grouse.

Dad took his 12 gauge shotgun, a bolt action J. C. Higgins®, and with four kids trailing him, he walked out of the yard in search of Ruffed Grouse. I was the oldest, so I got to walk right behind him in the most important position.

"Dad," I said, "Larry and I heard a speeder behind the barn again. We looked for it, but we couldn't find it." I thought that he might want to help us look for it. Now that we had a gun it would make it more interesting.

"I don't think we'll bother with him for now," Dad replied and we continued on past the barn and through the small field to the south. We were approaching another stand of spruce when wop.....wop....wop...wop...wop...wop.. wop wop whirrrrr. The sound erupted from within the stand of spruce.

"There Dad, there!" I shouted. "Listen, I hear another speeder. It's right there Dad, in them spruce, right over there. Did ya hear it Dad, did ya?"

"I heard it son, now you kids, just be quiet for a minute or two."

I followed very closely in my father's footsteps, my brother and sisters sneaking along behind me, as he cautiously moved forward a few steps at a time, halting and searching the surrounding bush for signs of his prey. Maybe that's why I could never find the speeder, I thought to myself. I always charged into the bush expecting to see this thing rolling down a set of railway tracks.

Dad was standing very still peering into the bush. I was holding my breath standing right behind him, trying to look around his body for a glimpse of what he was looking for when suddenly wop....wop....wop...wop...wop.. wop..wopwop whirrrrr. My heart was pounding a mile a minute at the sound. The speeder was so close I just knew that this time, thanks to Dad, I was going to see it.

Not looking up, I tugged at Dad's jacket. "Did you hear the speeder?" I whispered to him. Moving his hand behind him he pushed my hand from his jacket and motioned for me to be quiet.

KABOOM.

I just about jumped right out of my skin at the sound of the shot. I had been so intent on getting a glimpse of the speeder that I hadn't noticed Dad raise the gun. I was not ready for the shot and it scared the dickens right out of me.

I looked at him, not wanting to believe what had just happened. "Did you shoot the speeder, Dad?" I asked, my voice quivering.

"I sure did," he said. "He's right over there by that log. You can go fetch him for me."

"Not me," I said. "I don't want to go get no shot speeder."

"Go fetch him," Dad said again. "He's dead. He can't hurt you."

Reluctantly, I walked towards the spruce trees. I didn't know what to expect, maybe a speeder with four steel wheels pointing skyward. What did a shot speeder look like anyway, I thought to myself.

As I approached the spruce trees, I noticed a bunch of feathers scattered around a log laying on the ground.

Laying in behind the log was a nice fat Ruffed Grouse.

I picked up the dead bird and noticed that it was quite warm. "You got a grouse," I shouted back to Dad. "You got a grouse." I forgot all about the speeder in the excitement of the moment.

Carrying the bird back to where my brother and sisters were, I hoisted it high so that everyone could admire Dad's kill and me, because I got to carry it.

"Well son," he said as I stood there admiring the bird, "there's your speeder."

I looked at him and back at the bird I was holding. Surely he was kidding me. This little grouse didn't look anything like a speeder.

Dad just laughed. He must have read the look of disbelief on my face.

"You see son, this is a boy grouse," he said. "In the spring of the year, these little guys pick themselves out a real nice log. Then they climb on top of it and they flap their wings real fast to make a noise that sounds just like a speeder. It's called 'drumming'. They do that to attract a female. But," and he winked, "what it really means, to us anyway, is I'm fat and ready for the pot. Come and get me."

As I pondered what Dad had just told me, I had visions of a little girl grouse being fooled like I was. In my mind I could just picture a lovesick grouse running down the railway tracks trying to catch a speeder.

BOBBY ADAMS IS A GIRL

There was only one school in Edson, a two-storey red brick building that everyone attended from grade one to twelve. The building sat right in the centre of the large school yard, which was divided in half by an imaginary line. Boys and girls were never allowed to mix in any activities outside of the classrooms.

Boys were assigned to the west side of the school and enjoyed the luxury of a large open school yard. Here on a very level, grassed surface they could play baseball, football, wrestle or do all the other masculine boy things.

The ground on the east side of the school was covered with fine gravel and shale. There was a small hill that ran north and south through the entire length of the yard. The hill and beyond were covered with numerous pine and spruce trees. Here, the girls could skip, play hopscotch and do other girl things among the tall spruce and pines.

There were three sets of doors leading into the school. The boys entered the school through the doors on the west side of the school and the girls entered through the doors on the east side. The doors on the south side of the school were never used. They were in no-man's-land and were the landmark that separated the boys from the girls.

Girls never played on the west side of the school and never entered through the west doors. Boys would never be caught dead playing on the east side of the school or entering through the east doors. If a real boy had to do something east of the school, he would go out to the street and walk around on the sidewalk rather than walk on the girls' side of the school.

In addition to his custodial duties, the janitor, a very big, tall man with a huge belly, was the enforcer, insuring that everyone stayed on the right side of the yard. To stray meant a visit to the office of the vice-principal, who was renowned for his ability to use the strap, and it was to him that the janitor carted any wayward souls.

"I think it's time that we found out a little about each of us," said our grade two teacher, Miss Palomar. "Who would like to go first?"

It was a brand new school year and show and tell time in the Grade 2A classroom in the Edson School House. I, like most every other kid in the classroom, would have nothing to show, but I was ready to tell the world about my family and our little farm. Hands were waving and flapping all around the room as many of my classmates tried desperately to get the teacher's attention. Those of us waving our hands wanted to be the first to tell her about ourselves, our families and our homes.

I learned the previous year that most things were done alphabetically and with the name of Adams, I had always been first. First for report cards, first for needles, first for all the things I had come to fear. This was one of the few times I wanted to be first. I waved my hand like I was a windmill. "Pick me," I cried to myself. "Pick me."

But Miss Palomar obviously didn't see my frantic efforts to draw attention to myself nor had she heard my silent pleas for recognition. She chose another for the honour of being first.

I slumped in my seat as I watched Margaret, little Miss-Know-It-All, the most obnoxious girl in the school, strut to the front of the class. There she stopped and said, "Thank you, Miss Palomar," in the sweetest little voice. I thought I would gag. Then she turned and gave the class a knowing smile that said, "I'm much better than you are."

In a voice that grated on my every nerve, she sneered. "My Daddy owns the biggest...he's got the best...he has the most..." and on and on she droned. I felt like I was going to be sick to my stomach by the time she finally finished and sashayed back to her seat. Not only was she obnoxious, I concluded, she was also hateful.

Several of my classmates had introduced themselves and relayed their family history before Miss Palomar happened to see me sitting at the head of the class, still waving madly.

"My name is Bob Adams," I proudly proclaimed as I stood before the class. "I live on a farm on the south road with my Mom and Dad. I have one brother, Larry, and two sisters, Gwen and Judy. I'm the oldest in the family. We live in a log house that my Dad built all by himself. We have three cows, an old sow and some baby pigs, two horses and a bunch of chickens. My Dad says that we have the best stump farm in the country," I proclaimed proudly.

"I see!" said Miss Palomar, looking a little puzzled. "Maybe you could tell the class what a 'stump farm' is and why yours is the best?"

"My Dad says that we have a good eighty acres of the best muskeg money can buy. The only thing that land is good for is growin' stumps. My Dad says that every time we cut down a tree for a post or firewood, we get ourselves another stump. Yup, my Dad says it's the best stump farm in the country," I beamed.

"I see," she replied, still smiling. "And what does your father do for a living if he's not a farmer?"

"He's a cat skinner," I proudly announced. I noticed immediately the change in Miss Palomar. She was no longer looking at me and smiling.

"I'm sorry, Bob," she said. "Could you tell the class again what it is that your father does for a living?"

"Yes, ma'am, he's a cat skinner," I repeated, speaking a little louder so the rest of the class was sure to hear. There, let Margaret, Miss Smarty Pants, beat that. Miss Palomar didn't ask her to repeat anything her Dad did. I'll bet her Dad couldn't even skin a cat, I chuckled to myself. "My Dad, he's one of the best cat skinners there is," I continued.

Miss Palomar was uneasy for the rest of the day. She gave me a funny look every time she talked to me. Something was bothering her and it must have hounded her all day. That night when I left school, I had a note from Miss Palomar to my mother asking if she could come to the school 'at her earliest convenience' for a meeting. Miss Palomar said in the note to Mom she suspected that I might be trying to impress my classmates by telling tall tales. She felt that it was important to get me straightened out before it got out of hand.

Mom wasn't too pleased with me when I brought the note home. She was sure that I had gotten into some type of trouble. Why else would the teacher want to meet with her? I hadn't seen Mom that worked up since I lost my boots in the mud. If there was trouble at school, then she wanted to know what it was. She was determined to get to the bottom of it before she met with Miss Palomar.

"Bobby, what did you tell Miss Palomar that would make her believe that you lied to her?" Mom demanded.

"I didn't tell any lies. Honest. I don't know why she wants to talk to you. I didn't do anything wrong," I wailed, as Mom pressed for information, to get some inkling as to why she had been summoned to the school house. It was a long evening. Mom never quit digging to get to the bottom of it.

First thing the next morning, Mom and I were on our way to the school house and coming from the farm we approached it from the east. Mom started through the trees on the east side of the school yard, but I dug in my heels. "We can't go in here," I protested. "This is the girls' side of the school. Boys aren't allowed to be on the girls' side. I'll get into big trouble if I get caught. The janitor is always watching, he'll kill me or take me to the vice-principal and I'll get the strap," I wailed.

Mom's obvious lack of concern for the sacred rules of the school shocked me. I just knew, walking through those trees, that I was not going to survive this day.

"I'll go in whichever side I please," Mom stated. She grabbed me by the arm and took off.

"No. Please, Mom," I wailed. "There's only girls on this side of the school. Please let me go around the other side and come in on the boys' side. Please, Mom."

"You're going with me, young man. Now I don't want to hear another word. Do you understand?"

"Please, Mom, please. It's the girls' side. Mom, please," I pleaded, but she was dragging me on through the trees. "Okay, Mom," I wailed. "I told a fib yesterday. I'm sorry."

That stopped her. "What fib did you tell?" She glared at me.

"I can't remember," I mumbled.

"Humph," Mom snorted, then turned and once more started for the school.

I prayed for God to strike me dead as we neared the small hill. I just knew someone was going to see me on the girl's side of the school. I was never so humiliated in my life. Here I was already in grade 2, being dragged to school by my mother and if that wasn't bad enough, she was taking me through the girls' side.

Then, the raspy whiny voice. I heard her before I saw her. "Bobby Adams is a girl! Bobby Adams is a girl!" She sang at the top of her lungs. "Look everybody, Bobby Adams is a girl. He's on the girls' side of the school." Oh God, I thought to myself. It's a fate worse than death. It's Margaret.

"Bobby Adams, shame on you. You're not supposed to be on the girls' side of this school," she shrieked in her snotty little voice. "You're in big trouble now."

Of all the people in the world, it had to be Margaret who saw me. At that moment, I knew, my mother didn't like me. She couldn't like me, or she wouldn't be dragging me through the girls' side of the school. I was in agony and now Margaret had fallen right in alongside of me and was matching my mother step for step. There was no place to hide. I was devastated.

At the top of the little hill, past the trees, along the east side of the school house most of the girls were skipping, but Margaret's whiny voice had alerted them to the fact that there was an intruder in their midst. They all stopped playing to watch. Mother was charging right through. I was trying to hide myself, disguise myself, anything to avoid the embarrassment. Margaret was whining. "I'm telling on you, Bobby Adams. I'll bet you get a good strapping. This is the girls' side and you're not supposed to be here."

Better the strap, I thought, than to have to listen to Margaret.

We arrived at the east doors. The final insult. My humiliation was complete. I was being forced to walk through the girls' doors. They needn't have opened them. Not for me, anyway. I felt so small. I knew that at that moment, I could have stood up straight to my full height and walked through the crack at the bottom of the door.

Without a second's hesitation, Mom flung the door open and with me in tow blew right past the janitor. He never said a word, but as the door slammed shut, I could still hear Margaret screeching. "I'm telling on you..."

Miss Palomar was very friendly as she greeted us. "Good morning, Bob," she smiled. "And you must be Mrs. Adams. My name is Miss Palomar, thank you for coming right in. Yesterday, in show and tell, I detected a small problem with the truth and I thought it best to get to the bottom of it." Miss Palomar wasn't wasting any time.

Mom never wasted any time, either. Miss Palomar hadn't heard the term 'cat skinner' before and she thought that my Dad actually skinned live cats for a living. Mom set her straight in short order, a cat skinner was a bulldozer driver and the two of them sat there laughing.

While I sat at my desk and sulked, Mom and Miss Palomar laughed about the misunderstanding. Ha ha ha, I thought to myself, as they enjoyed their little laugh. No one cared about me.

Mom left the school when the bell rang. Lucky me, I got to stay in the classroom and watch my classmates file in and take their seats.

"Good morning, class," said Miss Palomar cheerily as Margaret frantically waved her hand to get noticed. "Yes, Margaret," she said.

Margaret stood up and turned to face the class. "Thank you, Miss Palomar," she cooed in the sweetest little voice. "I want to report Bobby Adams for..."

I slouched as low as I could in my seat, hoping that a big hole would open and I'd be swallowed up.

THERE'S NOTHING LIKE A GOOD CEEGAR

It was not often that any of us kids were left on the farm while the rest of the family went to town, but on this day, Larry and I were left at home. There were chores to do, and since they were not done, our fate was to stay home and do them. It was a lesson that in the future, if we wanted to go to town with the rest of the family, we would be sure to have our chores done ahead of time.

We finished the chores and set out to entertain ourselves. We played with the puppies, we played some marbles and were having a fairly good time in the dirt pile by the outhouse. We finally tired of building roads and hauling dirt up and down the heap of clay and looked for other sources of amusement.

"I know, let's take one of Grandpa Adams' cigars and smoke it," I said.

"What'll he say if we get caught?" Larry asked.

"He's got so many, he won't know the difference," I replied. "Anyway, we did a pretty good day's work already and Grandpa always says, 'there's nothing like a good ceegar after a hard day's work'."

"I want my own," Larry piped up. "I don't want to share and anyways, Grandpa always smokes a whole one."

"We can take two as easy as one," I answered and we took off for the house.

Grandpa always had a couple of big wooden boxes of White Owl® cigars. We found one of them on the cupboard in the kitchen. It had been opened and about half the cigars were gone.

"I bet he won't even know we took them out of here," I said as we each scooped our own cigar and some matches.

"Where we gonna smoke them?" Larry asked.

"I dunno, think we should go into the toilet where no one can see us?"

"It stinks too much in there," he said, curling his nose at the thought.

"What about the woodshed? No one will see us in there."

"Good idea," he replied, as we took our ill-gotten booty and ran to the woodshed.

We would share the woodshed with Bunny, our Fox Terrier. She had a litter of pups and had claimed a corner where she and the pups were out of the way.

We sat on the dirt floor among the wood chips and the sawdust, our backs to the wall, and peeled the band off the cigars.

"Now that smells like a real ceegar," I said as I passed the length under my nose, feeling the scent of the strong tobacco in my nostrils. I was very careful to make certain that I was following the exact procedure that Grandpa always followed. I aped him to a T.

Grandpa always bit the end off the cigar before he lit up. This was another important step in the manly art of cigar smoking. We both chewed away and pulled on the end of our cigars. Finally, my cigar looked like it had been mashed on the wall. It was almost ready, however, no self-respecting cigar smoker would think of lighting up without first tasting his cigar. I wrapped my tongue around the cigar and pulled it along my lips. I sat back and looked at the cigar, wet with saliva. "Man, did that taste good," I crowed.

It was time to strike the match. Time to light the ceegar. Ah, but it felt good to be so grown-up.

With the chewed-up end of the cigar in my mouth I touched the lighted match to the other end and sucked vigorously. Too vigorously, perhaps. A sudden rush of smoke charged through the cigar, past my lips and down my throat so rapidly I barely had time to react before a fit of coughing overtook me. This sudden change of events in my body was obviously too much for my eyes and they began to water profusely.

Larry was laughing his head off as he watched me double over in agony, coughing uncontrollably with tears streaming down my cheeks. "That's the funniest thing I ever saw!" he howled. "Could you do that again, Rob? I'd like to see it one more time. I think there was smoke coming out of your ears."

"Watch that first puff," I squeaked at him. "It sort of sneaked up on me. I thought I was gonna choke to death."

Larry lit his cigar and was much less exuberant than I was. He took nice short puffs and sat there blowing smoke like an old pro. I was still having trouble breathing.

"Ah yes," said Larry, "there's sure nothin' like a good ceegar after a hard day's work." He took a good drag, being very careful not to inhale.

My coughing must have attracted the pups for they had wandered over and were playing around. One of them was growling and tugging on my pant leg.

We sat there, the two of us, puffing on our cigars and talking big people talk. Mostly we boasted about how good a real cigar tasted. For some reason, I had suddenly taken to coughing a lot, and each drag on the cigar would trigger another bout and more tears. My eyes felt like I had spent the entire afternoon bawling my head off.

The pups were just learning to drink from a dish and they ran around us, pulling at our pant cuffs and growling. They were enjoying our company and they provided a lot of laughs as they tumbled over themselves.

I started to lose interest in the pups when I thought I saw the door to the woodshed go whizzing by. "You feel a little dizzy?" I asked Larry as I searched for the runaway door.

"Yeah, and a little sick to my stomach. I think maybe we worked too hard this morning."

"Could be. You know Grandpa never smokes these things all the way down. He takes a few puffs and then let's them go out an' chews on 'em for awhile. I feel a little sick to my stomach, too. Think maybe I'll just chew on mine for awhile."

We each watched our cigars as the smoke trailed to a thin wisp and then disappeared. When it was dead, we chewed. Then we chewed some more.

"Think we ought to light up again?" I asked. "I don't feel any better doing this. In fact I think it's gettin' worse."

"Me too," he replied. We struck another match.

My head was spinning. My stomach was about two revolutions behind it. "I think I'm feeling better now that I'm lit up again. What do you think?" I spoke a little louder to show more strength.

"I think I'm going to puke," Larry said.

"Don't do that," I said. "Then you'll really be sick. Hey,

I know what's missing," and I started to feel a little better.

"What's that?" Larry moaned.

"Well, Grandpa never gets sick when he smokes ceegar's, does he?"

"No."

"Know why?" I asked, feeling quite cocky now.

"No, I don't think so," groaned Larry.

"Because he always has a beer with his ceegar. And guess what?"

"What?" he asked.

"I know where he keeps his beer. Want one? I'm gonna get one and settle my stomach."

"Sure. I can't feel any worse."

Out of the woodshed I stumbled, into the fresh air, heading for the house.

"There you go," I handed Larry his beer with a big horseshoe and buffalo head on the label.

We toasted each other and had a swig.

I thought it would be better to follow Grandpa's example here, so I took a puff and then threw back a good swig of beer. But something got mixed up in there. The beer tried to push the smoke down, while my throat decided enough was enough and was pushing both back up. I kept my mouth shut and tried to swallow, but the beer started to fizz and the bubbles were coming out my nose. I coughed and spewed beer and smoke all over the front of me and on the pups. I had beer and snot running down my face. I couldn't stop coughing and my eyes were watering like crazy.

"That's more like it," Larry said, setting his bottle down and grinning at me. "I feel better now. How about you? You don't look so good, Rob," he observed.

"Oh God, I feel like hell," I moaned quietly to myself as

I tried to wipe the tears, the beer and the snot off my face.

"Hey, look at that pup licking the top of your bottle," I said, trying to concentrate on anything but how I felt. We both watched as the little black-and-white male puppy we had named Spot gave the top of the bottle a real going-over with his tongue.

"He really likes it, doesn't he?" Larry commented. "Think he'd like some of his own?"

"He can have some of mine," I offered. "Let's pour some in his dish. Maybe they'd all like some. Maybe they're beer drinking dogs just like us."

"Ha ha ha," we both laughed and poured some beer into the dogs' dish.

Spot loved his beer. The other two puppies had a little and then left to pull at pant legs. Spot's enthusiasm for the beer took our minds off ourselves for a few minutes. He stuck his nose in the dish and lapped up beer like there was no tomorrow. Every once in awhile, he would lift his head up and bark. YIP YIP YIP YIP. Pretty soon he would take a lick of beer, then yip at the dish. He even tried to yip with his nose stuck in the beer.

"What's Spot barking at now?" Larry asked. Spot had finished his beer and was heading for the corner of the woodshed, barking his little head off. Barking at nothing. He was barking in the direction of his dish and backing towards the corner of the shed. He kept barking and backing up until he had worked himself right into the corner. His stubby little legs continued to push, trying to back up further. He kept on yapping and pushing. Spot was going nowhere fast.

"Looks to me like Spot is drunk," Larry observed.

"Tighter'n a nit, I think." We both roared with laughter, had another swig and a good pull on the cigar.

"I don't think this beer is the answer, either," I said to Larry. "I think I'm gonna puke. How do you feel?"

"I'm sick. I think I'm gonna die."

"We gotta hide these beer bottles and these ceegars. If Mom finds them, she'll skin us alive," I mumbled the obvious.

"Let's go back in the trees," he replied. "We can hide them there. Nobody'll ever find them."

We made it to a stand of small spruce trees behind the woodshed and there on all fours proceeded to heave our guts out. Man, I was never so sick in all my life. There was no comfort in knowing that my brother was just as sick. Grandpa must have done something different because he never got sick. I'd have to watch him closer, if I lived, that is.

"Maybe we got a couple of green beers," I said to Larry as we lay on the ground in the spruce trees.

"How do you figure that?" he groaned.

"Well, sometimes in the morning when Grandpa is sick, I've heard him tell Dad that he must have got a green beer last night."

"Isn't that just our luck," he moaned. "Two green beers in one case."

TINNICK, TINNICK, TINNICK

"It's an electric fence," Grandfather said as he proudly showed off the latest addition to his farm. "You hear that tickin' in the box?" I leaned a little closer with everyone else and sure enough I could hear it. Tinnick. Tinnick. Tinnick went the little black box just as regular as clockwork. "It'll keep the horses and the cows in. I even put it around the pig pens. Some of those old sows have a tendency to want to roam a bit."

We all stood there looking at the single strand of wire that stretched along the top of the fence, all the way to the corner of the field and down the side before disappearing into the trees and out of sight. At the top of every post, Grandfather had nailed a small porcelain insulator and the wire ran from insulator to insulator. "You can't let the wire touch anythin' but them insulators or it'll ground out and won't work," he explained.

"Here, boy," he said to me. Grandfather always called me 'boy'. "Come over here and give me a hand. Just for a minute. I want to show you somethin'."

When he called me, my chest jumped out so far I just

about popped every button off my shirt. I strutted over and stood beside him like I was a king or something. Grandfather was always the centre of attention and when you helped Grandfather, the spotlight shone on you. I was very happy that he had asked me to help. He could have asked anyone, but he chose me. I was feeling real proud as I stood next to him and waited for instructions.

"Now I want you to take a hold of this wire for a sec," he said, as he pointed to the exact spot on the hot wire where he wanted me to grab it. "C'mon boy, it won't bite you," he said encouragingly.

I didn't really need much encouraging, not when I had a chance to help Grandfather, especially in front of everyone else. As they stood around watching me with envy, I reached forward and grabbed hold of the wire real tight, at the same time looking at Grandfather for his approval.

ZAP.

My whole body jolted immediately. My hair stood on end and my eyes about bugged right out of my head. "Let go!" my head yelled at my hand. "Let go, you fool!"

ZAP.

Man, I was nailed again. Now my whole body jerked and was starting to tingle. Again my head yelled for my hand to let go.

ZAP.

Once more the current surged through my hand, up my arm and across my shoulders. My head jerked back as the current plunged down the length of my body and through my legs. I could feel my toes curl inside my shoes.

Three times. Three times I got zapped before my hand obeyed the rest of my body and let go of that lousy wire. I couldn't believe I held on that long.

I stood there in a trance. I was completely stunned. "What happened?" I stammered and looked around. My hair was still standing on end and my eyes were as big as saucers, bugged right out of my head. I was completely stunned—not scared—I didn't know what had happened.

I looked at Grandfather to see if I had done something wrong and he was doubled over laughing. He slapped his knee. "Har har har Ooooeeeeyy," he roared. "Boy, if you could only see the look on your face right now. I got you a good one. Did you see the look on his face?" he asked the others. "Man, that was priceless."

Everyone else was having a good belly laugh at my expense.

Then Grandfather opened the control box to show us the inside and the battery that provided the power. Tinnick. Tinnick. Tinnick went the timer in the control box. Every time it ticked, it sent an electric current through the wire. If you touched the wire, the current sent a shock through you. I could vouch for the shock. My hair was still standing on end and my arm kept tingling.

That electric fence was a great source of amusement and frustration to my grandfather. It would make his day whenever someone new came to the farm and he was able to introduce them to his electric fence. Every time someone would grab the wire and get a shock, he would just roar with laughter.

"Cows, pigs, kids, everybody an' everythin' respects that fence, everythin' but my horses," Grandfather lamented. I stood beside Grandfather and felt his pain as we both stared at the broken wire. He shut off the power and repaired the electric fence. "It's them horses alright!" he crabbed. "They tear down this fence every night. It's no respect. No respect I tell you." Those stupid horses created no end of frustration for Grandfather as they seemed to be oblivious to his charged-up fence.

"How come you got them chains hanging from the horses' necks?" I asked Grandfather when I noticed that all his horses sported new neckwear. A small length of chain was hanging from each neck. The chain could have been attached to the halter, but it wasn't. It was actually hanging from a piece of heavy wire strung around their necks.

"I've got their number, boy!" he chuckled. "I've got their number now." Grandfather was back to his normal happy self. "Them horses won't be tearin' down that fence no more."

That sure didn't make a whole lot of sense to me. "Why do you need the chain to keep them away from the fence?" I asked.

"Them horses, they think they're pretty smart," said Grandfather. "They know that if they put their nose on the wire they'll get a shock. They've taken to puttin' their heads over the wire and leanin' on it. They keep breakin' the darn wire before they get the shock. Now, when they start to put their heads over the fence, the chain touches the wire and they get a shock before they can break the wire. Boy you should see them horses jump and snort when the chain touches that wire. Their tails stick straight out behind them and they race back to the centre of the field. When they stop runnin' they stand there and look at that fence. They can't figure out what's happenin'," he laughed and slapped his knee. I watched Grandfather real close to make sure that I had that knee-slappin' bit down pat.

"But I don't ever see any of them at the fence no more," I said.

"That's right," said Grandfather. "I think they get a better jolt from that chain and they've got enough shocks now to know to stay back."

Grandfather was so happy in describing how those horses got zapped that I wasn't sure of his motive. I kept wondering if the fence was there to keep the horses in or just to zap them for Grandfather's amusement.

I always made it a point to be at Grandfather's if company was coming. I knew for a fact that any newcomer was a candidate for that fence and I wanted to be standing right beside Grandfather when someone would ultimately grab the wire. Grandfather was always standing right where he could watch their eyes bug out and their hair stand on end. It was at those times that I knew what Grandfather had meant when he said to me "Boy, if you could only see the look on your face right now." I saw that look on many faces. Every time I saw it, I would roar right along with Grandfather. The knee slapping was the sign that it had been a good ZAPPING. Grandfather was the ultimate prankster. Life was never dull when he was around.

"No way," my cousin said. "I know that I'll get a shock if I touch that wire. You can't fool me. Mom told me to be careful, that you'd try to trick me." My cousin was the ultimate test for Grandfather. The news of the fence had gotten around the neighbourhood and town. My cousin, like many others, had been warned to watch out for Grandfather and his electric fence.

"You're too smart for me," Grandfather said after exhausting his bag of tricks and my cousin not getting within forty feet of the fence. "I guess I can't trick you, can I? Come on, boys, and help me call the pigs. I don't have time to fool around now, it's feedin' time."

With that we were all off to the hog pens to help Grandfather call the pigs in.

"Suueeyy suueeyy suueeyy," yelled Grandfather when

we got to the pens. It was the dinner call and the pigs all came running up to the troughs. Pigs were squealing and pushing against one another as they vied for a place at the trough. Grandfather was very carefully looking them over. There was something wrong near the back of the troughs.

"Here, boy," he said, handing my cousin a pail of water. Grandfather never had to remember anybody's name. To him they were either boy or girl. "Hold this. I'm goin' to need some help to scare them pigs. There's somethin' wrong with those pigs and I can't see the ones in the back. Now just give me a minute, let me get over to the corner," he instructed my cousin. He walked about fifteen feet down the fence line and again looked very hard at the pigs.

"No," he said. "I just can't see those ones at the back. We'll have to scare those pigs in the front and get them out of the way. When I yell, you just pour a little water on the fence and see if that'll move 'em."

Very carefully, my cousin picked up the pail of water and watching Grandfather to make sure he didn't make a mistake, he lifted it above the fence.

"Maybe you'd better move down here a bit," Grandfather was giving him very explicit instructions. "Are you right in front of those big sows?" he asked.

"I am now," said my cousin.

"Okay. Now," yelled Grandfather.

I could see the pail tilt in my cousin's hands and the water starting to pour out. It was like watching slow motion. The mouth of the pail tilted slowly towards the fence. A small trickle of water dripped over the rim and ran down the side of the pail. It missed the fence by a good foot.

"More water," yelled Grandfather. "Pour faster."

Grandfather's yell startled my cousin and the small stream of water suddenly became a gusher that poured over the wire. There was no need for further instruction.

"Yeow!" screamed my cousin, as the pail flew from his hands sending water flying in every direction. The water pouring didn't scare the pigs, but that blood curdling scream and the flying pail sure the heck did. Pigs squealed and ran for cover away from the fence.

My cousin stood there. He was soaking wet. His hair was standing on end and his eyes were bugging out as he tried to figure out what happened to him.

"Har har har," roared Grandfather, as he doubled over with laughter and slapped his knee.

"Har har har," I roared along with Grandfather, keeping a close eye on him. I noticed that I got everything just right. I doubled over at just the right time and slapped my knee exactly the way Grandfather did. "We sure got him, didn't we, Grandfather?" I could barely contain myself. I was as happy as he was.

"We sure did, boy!" Grandfather was still laughing as we walked away. He sure liked a good joke, I thought.

My poor cousin wasn't sure what hit him. He was still standing there in total disbelief. His eyes were as wide as saucers and his hair was sticking out in every direction. On top of it all, he was soaking wet. Most of the water upon leaving the pail had found its way to him. He sure was a sorry sight.

"Who do you think we should get next?" I asked Grandfather. I knew there would be a next victim and I didn't want to miss it.

"I don't know, boy," he said. "It's getting tough." He thought for a while, then a devilish smile crossed his face. "Maybe we should try to get Ma. What do you think?"

"Boy, that would be great," I said, as I envisioned Ma, a very large lady, grabbing the hot wire. Ma's hair was always done up in a bun with bobby pins holding it in place. I could just see her hair shooting straight out from her head with electric sparks flying from the bobby pins. "How we gonna do that, Grandfather?"

"You leave that to me, boy," he smiled fiendishly and winked at me. "It'll be our little secret."

"You bet, Grandfather," I replied without having any idea of what he was going to do. One thing I knew for sure, I wanted to be a part of this show. I wouldn't miss it for anything.

All the way home from Grandfather's place, I thought of Ma grabbing that wire. By the time I got home, I could hardly wait for the next day, Ma's day with the wire. It would be a day to remember, I thought to myself.

That night I was telling Dad how Grandfather had tricked my cousin. "You should have seen him. He wouldn't grab the wire, so Grandfather got him to pour water on the pig fence. The water pail went flying and the pigs were running and squealing." I got excited just reliving the experience.

"He's still playing around with that, is he?" Dad laughed.

"Uh huh," I said. I was so excited that I couldn't contain my secret any longer. "Guess who Grandfather's gonna get next with the electric fence?"

"I don't know. Who's he gonna get next?" Dad asked, still smiling.

"You can't tell anyone," I said. "It's a secret."

"I think you can tell me."

"Promise not to tell?"

"I promise."

I looked around the room to see if anyone was watching or listening. "We're gonna get Ma," I whispered.

"Are you now," Dad said and the tone in his voice suddenly changed. For the first time he seemed genuinely interested. "And who's idea was this?"

I looked around the room again. I sure wanted to take credit for this great idea. "It was Grandfather's idea," I said rather dejectedly.

"Well, we'll just have to see about that," Dad said and he was very serious.

"You're not going to tell Grandfather that I told you, are you, Dad?" I didn't want Grandfather to think that I was the kind of helper that couldn't keep a secret.

"You can count on that," Dad said.

The next day there was a whole bunch of us at Grandfather's place, which was not unusual for it was the hub of activity. Everyone was busy and Grandfather was in his glory giving directions and telling stories. As usual he was the centre of attention.

This would be the perfect day to get Ma, I thought. Almost everyone was there and they would all see her get jolted. I could hardly contain myself.

The day wore on and I stuck to Grandfather like glue. I wasn't going to miss this for anything. If I asked him once, I must have asked a thousand times, "Are we gonna get Ma today?"

He'd just wink at me and give me a knowing nod.

This was the day, I just knew it. I could feel the excitement in the air.

Ma was a great cook and she cooked a delicious supper. I was so excited, I could hardly eat. Everyone who had been there that day stayed for supper. "I bet they know that Grandfather's going to get Ma today, too," I thought to myself.

After supper, it was time to feed the pigs. All the men

got up and thanked Ma for a delicious meal and left with Grandfather to go 'slop the hogs.' Dad had helped Grandfather earlier in the day and a big fire had been lit under the caldron. The pigs' supper had been cooking while we ate. It was boiling pretty good when we got there.

Everybody went over and stood by the pig pens and the troughs. Everybody, that is, except Grandfather. I stayed close to him and watched.

"Are we gonna get Ma now?" I whispered to Grandfather, so that no one else could hear.

"You just stay close and watch," he winked at me and grinned.

Like a shadow, I followed Grandfather. Over at the cauldron, I watched every move that Grandfather made. He was busy getting everything ready to feed the pigs. The mash was boiled and was ready to be dumped into the troughs. It was scooped from the cauldron with a five gallon pail and carried by hand over to the pens where it was poured into the troughs. Everything was ready. It was time to feed and Grandfather called for help since there was lots of help standing around. But everyone was too busy talking. They paid him no heed.

Grandfather didn't like to be ignored. "What's a son-in-law good for if he won't help an old man?" He winked at me.

"I'll help you, Grandfather," I offered.

"You're a little too small to carry these heavy pails, boy," he said and walked over to where the pails were stacked. A length of chain was hanging from a branch, dangling right in front of the pails and he casually grabbed it to throw it to the side.

ZAP.

Grandfather's tweed cap flew off and landed on the

ground, revealing his head, which except for a fringe of hair around the sides and the back was bald as a billiard ball. When that cap left his head that fringe stood on end and his eyes bugged out.

I was standing right there looking into his face when that cap exploded from his head. My jaw dropped. I was as surprised as Grandfather. I swear I could see little electric charges dancing through that fringe of hair. I had an instant flashback to my own experience with the wire.

We both stood there motionless, frozen in time. There was Grandfather, my idol, the king of the pranksters, getting his just due. He had a stupid, stunned look on his face.

ZAP.

He was nailed again and his whole body jerked as the current surged through him once more. My body jerked too and I recoiled back, not from the shock, but in surprise. A smile started to creep over my face as I realized what was happening. "Hang on Grandfather," I yelled, hoping for at least three jolts.

ZAP.

Grandfather jerked again, dropped the chain and stood up straight like he had sat just on a nail. He let out the most blood curdling "AAYYYYIIIEEE" that I had ever heard.

He had let go of the chain and was doing a little jig around in front of the cauldron. There was no laughing, no knee slapping from Grandfather this time, although he was cussin' pretty good and shaking his hand like he was trying to get something off it. It was the tingling, I knew the feeling.

I couldn't help it, the king of the pranksters was putting on a better show than any I had seen before. I started to laugh.

"Har har har," I heard the sound of others laughing and looked up to see the rest of the men standing by the pens as they enjoyed this turn of events.

"Har har har." There was more laughter and I realized that the women had suddenly appeared up at the house. Ma was standing right in the middle of them laughing the hardest.

"Har har har," I roared right along with the rest of the men. "We sure got you, didn't we, Grandfather?" I said and slapped my knee in the approved fashion.

When the laughter died down, I got to thinking. That chain didn't belong there, so I went over to examine it. It was still hanging there, right where Grandfather had let it go. It looked suspiciously like the ones around the horses' necks. It was attached to a piece of wire, hanging from a branch. I noticed that an insulator had been attached to the branch. The wire ran from there over to the fence.

"I wouldn't touch that chain if I was you, Bob." I looked up. Dad stood behind me with a big grin on his face.

OUR BIFFY IS A TWO-HOLER

"How deep do we have to dig?" I asked Dad. I was on the shovel at the bottom of the hole throwing the thick heavy clay out the top and onto the pile.

"You've got a ways to go yet. You take 'er down as far as you can and then I'll finish up. It's got to be 6-8 feet deep."

We were in the process of digging a new hole for our outhouse. Our land was flat and we didn't have a knoll or small hill on which to put this necessity. There were no large clearings either, so our old outhouse had been placed back in the bush. But it was too far from the house and it scared a lot of people when they had to go back there, particularly at night.

The new location was going to be right beside the woodshed, only about twenty feet from the house, so it wouldn't be too far to walk. I dug until I encountered difficulty throwing the clay out of the hole. Dad came over to see how I was doing just as I threw a shovelful up towards the mound of clay piling up around the hole. The clay landed on the side of the pile and then came thundering back down, bringing more with it. As chunks of clay came raining down on me, I put my hands over my head to keep from getting hit. "You better let me take over," he said. "I think there's more going back down the hole than you're throwing out."

"Okay," Dad said when he had finished digging the hole to the desired depth. "Now that we have a new hole, we have a choice. We can move the old toilet over here or we can build a new one. What'll it be?"

That was an easy decision; we all voted for a new toilet.

"We're going to need some lumber then," Dad responded to our decision. "Do you think we can rustle up enough lumber to build 'er?"

"You betcha," I answered, not having a clue where we would find any lumber, let alone enough to build a toilet. "Where we gonna get the lumber, Dad?" I asked after thinking about it for a minute.

"What say we mosey on over to the sawmill and see what's laying around."

Just south of our place was a mill site and we walked over to see if they had any cull lumber that we could scrounge.

"Well look at this. I'd say these look like some pretty good boards right here," Dad commented, standing beside the slab pile that contained both slabs and cull lumber. He started into the pile. "Let's dig through these and see if we can come up with enough usable boards to build us an outhouse."

The boards were an assortment of 2" x 4", 2" x 6", 1" x 4", 1" x 6" and 1" x 8" and were a variety of lengths. Many looked like perfectly good boards on one end, but at some point along their length they turned into slivery slabs.

Actually all of the boards were rather slivery as the lumber was all rough-cut. None of it had been put through the planer.

When Dad figured that we had close to enough, he told me to continue to dig out some more. He would go home, get the horses, the wagon and return.

I stayed at the site and worked at getting more boards out of the pile, but they were quite a bit heavier now that Dad wasn't helping. I never paid any attention to how the boards were piled when Dad was there, but now that he was gone, I realized that none of these stupid boards or slabs were stacked. They had been thrown out willy-nilly and were a terrible tangled mess. I found one board that I thought looked pretty good, but it was stuck or lodged under a pile of others. I was having a devil of a time trying to free it and had worked up quite a sweat by the time Dad returned. It was a board we didn't need, but he thanked me for helping and dislodged it with little effort. Dad had a tremendous amount of patience. I, on the other hand, was tired and frustrated. I was ready for a rest.

"I wanna pound the nails in," I stated, as Dad measured and sawed the boards into the proper lengths. Then, as every board was ready to be nailed on, he would hold the boards in place and I would hammer away, hitting the boards as often or more than I hit the nails. Eventually they were all driven home. The outhouse sitting above the new hole was framed and the walls sheeted with boards of a variety of widths.

"Are we gonna cut a moon in the door?" I asked.

"Nope. No need to. This lumber is pretty green. When it dries there will be cracks between the boards big enough to drive a truck through. There'll be enough light coming in then. There'll be no need for a moon."

When the outhouse was framed, it looked like any other building.

"Now we need a couple of smooth boards for the seats. We don't want the womenfolk to get a sliver in their behinds when they sit themselves down, now do we?" Dad grinned as he went into the woodshed and returned a few minutes later with a couple of smooth boards. First he measured and cut the board for the back part of the seat.

"Here you go, you can nail this on. Try to hit the nails and not the wood. We don't want to have any rough spots," he winked.

While I hammered on the first board, Dad measured and cut the second, which I grabbed. I was on a roll. The first one went on real easy and I didn't hit the board once.

"Whoa up. We have to cut the holes in first. It's much easier if you cut half the hole that goes in the first board before you nail the second board on," Dad cautioned me.

I watched in amazement as Dad very carefully measured out and cut not one but two half-circle holes out of the first board. "Okay. Now you can nail the other board on."

When I had completed my task, pounding the nails into the second board, Dad finished up, measuring and cutting the last of the holes. I was amazed. There on our toilet seat were two holes, perfect circles. Folks using our toilet would have a choice. Dad then took a wood rasp and rounded the edges of both holes. He finished smoothing them off with sandpaper.

"Well, what do you think?" he asked when he had completed the last task.

"Wow! Our biffy is a two-holer. I bet nobody else has a two-holer. Wait till I tell Mom. I bet she'll be surprised. Hey Mom," I yelled as I ran to the house, "come see our toilet. It's a two-holer."

I was never sure why there were two holes because only one person ever visited our toilet at any one time. It was certainly not a place where one would want to sit for too long. There was no loitering in the bathroom in those days. In the summer, the smell and flies would drive you out and in the winter, it was just too dang cold. If there was a slight breeze blowing in the winter, you could be assured that there would be a gale whistling through the cracks into the outhouse. The wind that came howling through those cracks would chill you to the bone. You risked frost bite if you stayed longer than was absolutely necessary.

Paper was a scarcity and always in great demand in the outhouse. The most common stock of paper was supplied by the Eaton's and Simpson's catalogues, with the shiny pages always the last to go.

From the inside of the outhouse, one could very easily keep track of the comings and goings on the farm. As Dad had said, the lumber was green when we put it up and as it dried, the boards had shrunk and some pretty good cracks had formed. While sitting on the throne, it was possible to see in every direction; the occupant had a good view of the entire area.

Our outhouse didn't have a moon carved in the door, but the interior was decorated with the best material available. Some of the magazines contained glossy pictures of the favourite movie stars of the day. My aunt always knew who the latest rage was and bought the magazines that contained the pictures of that star. Once the magazine had been read and reread the pictures would be saved and taken to the outhouse where they would be pasted to the walls. Yessiree, normal decorations or wallpaper had no place in our outhouse. We had the best. We had the faces of movie stars.

During a visit to our outhouse one could not help but dream of their favourite star. I would see the faces of the various stars that adorned the walls of our outhouse: Roy Rogers, Gene Autry, Errol Flynn, Jane Russell and Marilyn Monroe. Man, to think of Marilyn Monroe smiling down on me, no doubt in approval, as I went about my business. It was easy to get carried away as I dreamed of things that would never be. No flies. No smell. Marilyn Monroe...It was almost enough to make one linger for just a few extra seconds. Well...almost.

I was coming home late one winter evening and as I turned into our yard, I stared in horror at our outhouse. It was glowing in the dark. It was on fire. I could see the flickering of the flames through the cracks in the walls. The yellow, orange and red tongues of the flames cast ominous shadows that raced and danced across the snow.

"Mom. Mom," I yelled as I raced towards the house. "The toilet's on fire! The toilet's on fire!"

As I got closer, I could see that the fire was not yet in the boards, but was down in the hole. Maybe we could save the building, if we hurried. In through the front door I burst and yelled again. "The toilet's on fire, Mom! The toilet's on fire!"

"Slow down. Slow down," said Mom quite calmly. "It's okay. Grandfather's here and he's just gone out to the toilet."

"But it's on fire! It's burning. I can see the flames. He'll be burned."

"No. It's not burning," she laughed. "That's just Grandfather. He likes to warm up the seat before he sits down. It's okay. Now come in and take off your coat. Everything's okay. Grandfather will be in when he's finished."

I wasn't too sure and I went to the window and looked out towards the outhouse. I could still see the glow of the flames through the cracks. They didn't appear to be getting any higher, but at that moment they didn't appear to be getting any lower, either.

I wasn't convinced that we weren't about to lose our outhouse and I stood at the window watching. I watched as the flames slowly died down and the glow retreated into the depths of the hole. There was the odd flicker and the light would suddenly flare up and then fade as the fire slowly died. Then it was dark. Shortly after the flames had died away, Grandfather came into the house as nonchalantly as if nothing had happened.

"What did Grandfather do out there?" I asked. "Why did he light a fire in the toilet? He could have burned down our brand new toilet and the woodshed and he could have burned down everything."

"Well," Mom said, "Grandfather doesn't like the cold very much and when he goes to the toilet, he likes to be warm. He lights a little fire; that's just his way of warming it up."

"How does he start the fire in the hole like that?" I had visions of him climbing down into the hole and lighting a fire, then climbing back out.

"He crumples up a piece of paper and then lights it and drops it into the hole."

"He could burn down the toilet! Couldn't he?"

"Yes, he could if he's not careful."

"I betcha I could light a fire in the hole and warm up the toilet when I have to go to the bathroom just like Grandfather does." Now I was envisioning a warm seat the next time I went.

"You most certainly will not, young man. If I ever catch

you lighting a fire in the outhouse you'll get your bottom warmed real good. Do I make myself clear?"

"Uh huh," I grumbled and thought of what it would be like to have a blaze under you while you went to the bathroom. Just think, with a nice little fire burning at the bottom of the hole, I could sit down and do my business in warmth and comfort just like Grandfather. I bet I could even see the pictures of the movie stars. I could imagine Roy Rogers with the shadows from the flames dancing across his face just like in the movies. And Marilyn Monroe...I could see her now...but that was another dream.

I don't think that Grandfather's derriere ever felt the cold bite of winter that lay in wait for the rest of us in the outhouse. Grandfather was a man whose needs were slightly ahead of his time; imagine indoor heating in an outhouse.

WHAT MORE COULD A YOUNG MAN ASK FOR?

Money was always in high demand and in very short supply in our house. Dad worked long hard hours and was often away from home for months at a time, working in the bush camps. He earned every cent he made.

I was always on the lookout for an extra penny. I would take on any extra chores or work for others if there was a chance of getting paid, but jobs were scarce, and good paying jobs were non-existent.

I watched the strange truck slow down as it neared our driveway, turn in and then idle towards the house. It was a brand new Ford with a long flat bed on it. The driver looked to be about Dad's age. He stopped and got out of the cab. "Is there a Bert Adams living here?" he asked me.

"Nope," I replied. "No Bert Adams here. Never heard of him."

"That's strange. I stopped by old man Ernst's place and he told me that Bert lived on the next place to the south. Way I figured it, this here's got to be the next place. You sure Bert doesn't live here?"

"I'm sure."

"What's your name, boy?"

I didn't think I liked this guy very much. "Bob," I replied.

"Bob what? You got a last name, boy?"

Now I knew I didn't like him. He sounded like a real smart-aleck. "Bob Adams," I mumbled so that he could hardly hear.

"So, you're Bert's boy, are you? Well Bobby, you just go tell your old Daddy that Jim's here to see him," he laughed.

It turned out that Dad and Jim were old friends. Jim hauled lumber from bush camps where Dad worked. They stood out in the yard talking about old times and laughing. All the while Jim called Dad, Bert.

It didn't make sense to me that Jim kept calling Dad, Bert and Dad didn't seem to object. I really didn't like Jim. He was a blowhard. He was loud and thought he knew everything. It didn't help that he didn't know Dad's real name, either.

After a while Dad said, "Come on in, I'll have the little woman put on some coffee and we'll discuss it some more."

As we walked towards the house, Jim reached over to tousle my hair. I dodged out of the way. I wasn't going to let him touch me.

"Tell me more about all this money I've got standin' around here just waiting to be harvested," Dad said, as we all sat at the kitchen table.

"Like I was saying, you're sitting on a gold mine here, Bert," Jim said and he waved his hand towards the living room.

We all looked at the living room. I could see the chesterfield, rocking chair, huge cabinet radio, coffee table and a gramophone. There didn't seem to be too much money standing around in there. Jim sure was full of it, I thought.

"How do you figure that?" Dad asked.

"Well, I'm told you've got a lot of Jack Pine on your land." He waved his arm towards the living room again, and I realized he was referring to the trees out back. "That's right, isn't it?" he asked.

"There's some pine on the back of the quarter," Dad replied.

"That's what I'm told." He sat back confidently and stuck his chest out. "I'm also told that they're just the right size...tall...straight...no limbs. That's ideal for telephone poles. Now, if what I'm told is correct, then we're in business. There's a real market for telephone poles on the prairie right now, Bert. Those farmers out there seem to have a lot of money now that the war's over and every house is getting a telephone. There's big money in telephone poles, if a man has a mind to put them up."

"Just how many of these telephone poles do you think they might want?" asked Dad.

"All you can provide, and then some," replied Jim. "Telephone poles is as good as gold right now," he laughed. "They're worth a buck a pole for twenty footers and two bucks for twenty-five footers.

"That's a lot of money for a pine pole," Dad whistled.

"I tell you Bert, they're as good as money in the bank. So how about it, you wanna get in on some of this easy money?"

"And just how do I go about pickin' all this money off my pine trees?" Dad had a little sparkle in his eye.

"You get them here to your yard and I'll pick them up and haul them. You don't have to touch them once they're ready for the road. That's my job. You need 100 poles per load, 90 twenty-footers and 10 twenty-five footers make up a load. I give you your money as soon as I count them. Before they're even loaded. That's cold hard cash, Bert. No cheques. No waiting till they're sold. Cash on the barrelhead."

"Sounds like an okay deal to me," whistled Dad. "That's a powerful lot of money. How come you need some five feet longer than the others?"

"Machinery, Bert, machinery. You wouldn't believe the size of some of them farm machines nowadays. The 25-footers are for the road crossings and the gates. The farmers have to be able to get their machinery under the wires so they need the extra height on the poles at those locations."

Jim sure could talk, he had an answer for everything.

"So, what do you say, Bert? Have we got a deal?"

"I'm not sure," Dad replied seriously. "It sounds like a lot of money, but I'm already working. I won't be able to put 'em up."

"What about the boys here?" Jim said, pointing to Larry and myself. "They look like a couple of strapping youngsters to me." Jim wasn't going to take no for an answer.

"I don't know," Dad said, looking at us. "What's all involved in getting the poles ready for the road?"

"They have to be cut to the proper lengths. The tops can't be less then four and a half inches across or more than five. Bring them to one location where I can get the truck to them, peel them and creosote the bottom five feet. Then sit back and collect your money."

That sounded pretty simple to me. All eyes were on Dad, waiting for his answer.

"Well boys," said Dad, addressing Larry and me, "I don't have time to take this on. How about it? Do you boys think that you'd like to take out a contract to do a little loggin' and bring in some telephone poles?"

"How much money do we get?" I asked. This was a rather dumb question, because we both cut a lot of firewood and we didn't get paid for that.

"Well, I don't know about that," said Dad. "What do you think it's worth?"

My brother and I looked at each other, at Dad and at the trucker. We had no idea what to ask for.

"How about you get a nickel a pole for every pole you get ready for the truck? That sound fair to you?" Jim volunteered. "And Bert here, he gets the rest for providing you with whatever you need."

I couldn't believe my ears. Did it sound fair, I thought, my mind racing back to last year when I got a job pickin' spuds. I could still remember that experience.

"You git two cents a bucket, and I expect each bucket to be full up. I wanna see spuds sticking out the top. Understand?" Henry growled at me.

"Yes sir," I replied, happy to have a job that paid real money.

"Okay then. Here's a bucket, now make sure it's full before you call it in to Emerson there." He handed me a five-gallon pail and pointed to Emerson, who was sitting on a pail out in the large potato field. There were about fifty kids scattered about him grubbing around in the dirt on their hands and knees digging the spuds out of the fresh turned earth.

"You can start right over there," Henry pointed out a row where a half a dozen others were already busy. "You work with them boys, they're my best crew."

I looked at my new crewmates. They were all three to four years older then me. I felt pretty important being assigned to work with them. I hustled over to my work place.

I was down on all fours digging out spuds. They could be found anywhere from a foot down to laying right on the surface. In my enthusiasm to impress Henry, I had dirt flying in every direction as I worked to maintain the standing of the group. Then a voice behind me called out, "Pail."

Emerson looked up. "Okay, Tom. Gotcha," he said.

Another voice called up from the other side of the work group, "Pail."

Emerson turned to see another person standing with a full pail of spuds. When a different voice behind me hollered "Pail," Emerson turned again to record the new voice. People were calling from all around him. Emerson sat in the middle spinning like a top as he identified and recorded each person and the fruits of his labour.

"Pail," a third voice called out from right behind me. Emerson recorded it, then turned to get the next caller. "Man," I thought, "these guys are really fast." My pail was only about half full of spuds and the last caller in my row was walking towards the bagging area. He hesitated right beside me and when Emerson turned the other way, quickly set his pail down beside me and grabbed my pail.

"Hey! That's my pail," I said keeping my voice as low as I could to avoid a scene. I grabbed for my pail.

"Shut up, stupid," the thief shot back. "Take my pail and call it in." He gave me a real dirty look.

"You stole my pail!" I said and started to get up.

"Take the full one, you dummy, and shut up or I'll shut you up," he growled at me.

Then the guy working ahead of me turned towards me and snapped, "Call that full pail in and bring it up here. And hurry up, you stupid turd."

I picked up the full pail of spuds and started walking.

"Pail," I yelled.

Emerson turned towards me. "Gotcha, Bob." Then he turned on another call.

I didn't get a chance to change pails, the guy waiting for it grabbed it from me and pushed me down beside his pail that was about three-quarters full. "Pail," he yelled.

I spent the rest of the day working the scam and worrying that I was going to get caught. I knew that I'd be in jail before the sun set.

"Let's see, Bob. Hmm." Henry was tallying up the numbers at the end of the day. From the way he was hesitating I could just feel that he knew I had cheated. I didn't pick half of those pails I called in. A guilty conscience is a terrible thing and I was having a terrible battle within myself. I couldn't look at Henry's face. "Thirty buckets. Not bad for the first day," he said. "You're a pretty good worker, Bob. I'm glad I put you with that good bunch there. You got a job here anytime you want it. Hope I'll see you tomorrow." He handed me sixty cents. It was more money then I had ever seen in my life.

I felt like crap as I held out my hand and took the money. "If I come back tomorrow, do I have to work with that group again?" I asked, looking at the ground and praying that he would say no.

"You betcha," Henry said. "Never break up a winning hand. See you tomorrow bright and early."

I walked home, and all the way I expected that Henry would drive up and ask me for the money back. The next day I was too sick to go to work. I never went back and I never forgot. I hadn't talked to Henry since. If I saw him on the sidewalk in town, I would walk across the street to avoid him.

Cutting telephone poles sounded real good to me. If I

cut poles, then picking spuds would be out of the question. Man, did I feel good about cutting telephone poles. Besides, I couldn't believe that I was going to be making all that money. A nickel a pole.

"It's a deal," we said and with that we entered into the logging business. Suddenly Jim didn't seem to be so bad. In fact, I was beginning to like him. I didn't even move when he reached over and tousled my hair.

"That's good men," he said. "We're gonna make a ton of money. You'll see."

"But, how are we going to get the telephone poles out of the bush after we cut them?" I asked Dad, suddenly remembering that they had to be brought out near the road for the truck.

"I guess we'll just have to get you a skid horse," Dad replied.

After Jim had left, I approached Mom, "How come Jim always called Dad, Bert?" I asked.

"Dad's family in Turner Valley have always called your father Bert," she replied. "He used to ride in rodeos before we got married and they felt that Bert sounded more like a cowboy's name than Bob did. When we go to visit them, you'll have to get used to it, because that's what they'll call him."

You could always depend on my Dad's word. If he said he was going to do something you could go to the bank on it. True to his word, a couple of days later, Dad called us out to the backyard.

Rounding the corner of the house, I stopped and stared. I couldn't believe my eyes.

"What do you think?" he said.

"I don't know. What is it?" I asked.

"He's your new skid horse, Barney," Dad smiled. "So

what do you think of him?"

I just stood there that morning staring at Barney. He was the saddest, poorest excuse for a horse that I had ever seen. His head hung almost to the ground, he was swaybacked and his eyes looked lifeless.

"Can he walk?" I asked.

"He's fine," Dad replied.

"He looks more like he's a candidate for the glue factory then a skid trail. Look at him, Dad, he looks sick." I walked around him. He didn't look any better from the back. "What's that?" I asked, looking at a sore on his hind leg.

The sore was about three inches across and it looked like it was moving. I looked closer and the whole area was a mass of movement. "Oh jeez Dad, that sore on his leg, look at it, it's got maggots crawling around in it. I think old Barney is half-dead already. He'll never be able to drag himself out of the barn, let alone a telephone pole out of the bush."

"Don't worry none about that," Dad said, showing no concern. "He's a good horse. We'll have him fixed up and ready to work in no time flat. He's a good skid horse. You'll see."

Dad led Barney down to the barn and tied him in a stall. He had some dark brown almost black-looking salve. Dad put large gobs of it on Barney's leg, then he treated his oats with different dark gunky stuff.

"What's that for?" I asked, as Dad poured the stuff on the oats and mixed it in.

"That'll get rid of his worms."

"You mean he's got worms as well as maggots?"

"I'm afraid so. He's been pretty badly neglected, but he'll be okay once we get him all treated up."

"With all the maggots and worms, maybe we should just

take him fishin'. We wouldn't have to look for bait." We all laughed.

Before too long, Barney started to show some signs of life in his eyes and his leg was all healed. His head still hung pretty low to the ground and he still had a swayback, but nobody could do anything about that. Barney was ready for work.

The area where we were cutting the telephone poles was about a quarter of a mile from our house. There was a nice stand of Jack Pine there. It was the same area where Dad got the logs to build our house, so there was a good skid trail back to the yard.

"You'll find that it works better with one of you at each location," Dad advised. "If one of you stays in the bush and the other stays at the yard, you can save a lot of time. Bob, you stay in the bush and cut the poles. Take Barney out with you in the morning and hitch him to a couple of poles, then send him in. Larry can stay at the house and when Barney comes in, he can unhitch him and send him back to the bush. Larry can peel poles while he's waiting for you to send Barney in with another load."

Barney, Larry and I made a good team. I took Barney with me out to the cutting area. I did most of the cutting of the poles and Larry did most of the peeling, however, we often worked together at one site or the other.

Dad was right about Barney, he was a good skid horse. Once he was hitched up to the poles, I would swat him on his butt and yell, "Yo Barney." With his head almost dragging on the ground and his back swayed, Barney would drag the poles back to the yard. I would stay in the bush and cut more poles.

Back at the house, Larry would unhitch the poles in the yard, then he'd swat Barney on the butt and yell, "Yo

Barney." Barney would return to the cutting area for another load. We never had to follow Barney one way or the other. He would spend his days going from the yard to the cutting area and back. Barney was indeed a good skid horse.

All the work was done by hand. We cut the poles by hand, using an axe and a swede saw. The swede saw looked like a metal bow with a saw blade instead of a drawstring. When using the swede saw, you always had to carry a bottle of kerosene with you to pour on the blade as the pitch from the pine trees would build and cause the blade to bind in the cut.

The best way to peel the poles was with an instrument called a draw knife. It had a long slightly curved blade with handles on both ends. Some handles followed the curve of the blade, others came straight back at you in a right angle. Standing beside the log you wanted to peel, you would reach ahead as far as you could, drop the blade into the bark and pull the knife towards you. This action would draw the knife under the bark and separate it from the wood.

Once we had a load of 90 twenty-footers and 10 twenty-five-footers cut, Larry and I would both concentrate on peeling them and putting creosote on the bottom five feet of every pole.

After the first load of poles was cut and ready for the road, we anxiously waited for Jim's return. Dad wasn't there when he made his appearance.

"That's okay," Jim said to Mom. "I can straighten up with Bert when I pick up the next load."

But Jim hadn't counted on Mom. He wasn't getting one pole until she got the money.

Undaunted, Jim first counted the poles and confirmed

that there were the required number. Then Mom counted out the money he handed her. "That's right," she confirmed. "One hundred and ten dollars for one hundred telephone poles. They're your poles now." She smiled and held the money tight in her hand.

Finally, it was time to sit back and relax. I could watch someone else work for a change. It was time for Jim to load the poles.

Man, I never knew that sitting back and relaxing could be such hard work. It turned out that Jim couldn't handle them poles by himself. I just about split a gut wrestling the small end of every one of those bloody poles onto that flat bed truck. Suddenly it came to me, the reason why I hadn't liked Jim when I first met him. He was a blowhard. As I was struggling on the ends of those poles, I knew I really didn't like him.

Larry and I were very busy little men and over the next three years we cut, skidded, peeled and creosoted many loads of telephone poles. For our efforts, our unwritten contract called for and we received the handsome sum of five cents per pole. We thought we were millionaires. Every time a load of poles sold and left that yard, we got five dollars. That is five dollars split two ways, $2.50 each.

What more could a young man ask for?

SOMETHING STINKS IN HERE

It was a trapline—a very small trapline—but it was my trapline. It covered parts of four different quarter sections, ours being one of them. The others were owned by neighbours who had no idea that I was running traps on their land. Asking their permission had never entered my mind. That they would have given their permission if asked had never been a question. To me, it was a God-given right to trap wherever there was a squirrel den.

"I could get a lot more squirrels if I had my own .22 and real Indian moccasins," I told Mom at the supper table one evening.

"If I've told you once, I've told you a million times, you're too young to be carrying a gun. Now I won't hear another word about it. As for the moccasins, I'd love to get them for you, but we just don't have the money. Maybe if you trap enough squirrels, you'll be able to buy some."

"But Mom," I argued, "if I had moccasins I could even wear them to school, then you wouldn't have to buy me any overshoes." I could just picture myself being the envy of every kid in the school when I showed up with real

Indian moccasins. I bet that no one else had even seen a pair, let alone owned any. I would be the toast of the school.

"You've got shoes for school. You've no need for moccasins," she said firmly.

I would often walk out of my way after school just for a chance to stop in at one of the local fur buyers. I would look at all of the different kinds of pelts they had hanging on the wall, stuffed in bags and even scattered about on the floor. But what I really went in to see was the genuine Indian moccasins.

The moccasins were always kept behind the counter, and the fur dealer, he knew that I coveted them. Every time I walked in, he would take a pair out of the showcase and lay them on the counter in front of me. They were made from tanned moose hide and were a nice golden colour.

"These moccasins are made by genuine Indians," the fur buyer would say. "Yes sir, they do everything themselves. The buck, he goes out and shoots the moose, then he skins it out and hauls it home. His squaw tans the hides and makes the moccasins. Them squaws, they chews that moose hide 'till it's soft, only way to tan it, you know. Then she smokes it to give it the colour and nice smell. Here son, have a feel of that." He handed me the moccasins.

I took them and could feel the softness of the leather. I didn't have to hold them to appreciate the strong smell of smoke. The whole place smelled the same as the moccasins, only much staler.

"Did you ever feel anything so soft, son?" he asked.

"No sir," I replied. "They sure are soft."

"How about that smell, did you ever smell anything nicer in your life?"

"It's got a pretty good smell," I had to admit. "As soon

as I get enough money, I'm gonna get me a pair of them," I told him.

"They'll be here, son. I've got a pair just your size. When you git enough money, you come back and see me. I'll save them, just for you."

Leaving the fur dealer's place, I ran for home, down to the CN Station, across the switch yard, over the many sets of tracks and through the bush until I got to Nick the Dog Man's place. There I slowed down and walked very carefully, not making any noise until I was past it, then ran the rest of the way home. I rushed through my chores and wolfed down my supper.

"Can I go and check some of my traps?" I asked Mom.

"Not anymore tonight. It's too dark and you're not going into the bush at night. You can check them on the weekend."

"Please, Mom," I begged. "There's no way that I can get home before it gets dark and those traps have been set since Sunday and haven't been checked yet." Dad had helped me set a half-a-dozen traps and the thought of a squirrel being in one of them was unbearable. I had to know.

"Well it's only Monday, they'll keep till the weekend. Now if I hear anymore about checking traps in the dark, you'll pick them up and there'll be no trapping."

No trapping was a fate worse than death. That was the key to me getting enough money to buy the moccasins. I would sulk in silence for the rest of the week.

Finally the weekend came. It was Saturday morning. I finished my chores without having to be asked and started out on the trapline.

The first trap was at a squirrel den in the stand of spruce and pine behind the barn. It was a small den and the trap was still set right where we had left it the week before. I followed the trail through the snow to the next stand of spruce and the next squirrel den, then the next, checking all six of my traps. At the end of the line, I had two squirrels.

They were frozen into the traps and I couldn't get them out so I picked up the trap and all and lugged everything home with me. I was on cloud nine when I walked through the door.

"I got two squirrels," I sang out and held them up for everyone to see.

"That's good, I'm proud of you," Mom said. "What are you going to do with them now?"

"I'm gonna skin 'em and stretch 'em," I said quite confidently.

"I see," Mom replied. "Do you know how to skin them and have you got any stretchers?"

"No," I replied, being jerked back to reality." Can you help me, Mom? Please," I begged.

"I'm sorry," she said. "Skinning squirrels is your father's job, not mine. He's skinned hundreds of them and I've seen him do it many times, but I don't know how. You'll just have to wait until he comes home."

"But I gotta get my traps back out. I can't catch squirrels if all my traps are in here."

"If you want the traps, then you'll just have to get them off the squirrels, or else wait until Dad gets home to do it for you."

"But he won't be home till Christmas," I wailed.

"Then you better quit talking and start working on getting them squirrels out of the traps."

I worked half the morning and finally succeeded in freeing the squirrels from the traps. I put the squirrels in the woodshed where they would stay frozen until Dad came home.

First thing Sunday morning I was up doing my chores again, anxious to get out on the trapline. While I was in the woodshed getting wood, I checked on my squirrels.

I charged into the house. "I need the gun, right now," I shouted to Mom. "I need Dad's big game rifle."

"What's the matter? What do you need the gun for?" she asked with a worried look on her face.

"I have to shoot those stupid cats," I shouted.

"I think you better slow down," Mom said, not looking nearly as worried as she had been a couple of seconds earlier. "Why do you have to shoot the cats?"

"Those stupid cats, they ate my squirrels," I whined with tears in my eyes. "There's nothing left of them. They're all gone."

"Well I don't think it's the cat's fault that you left the squirrels where they could get at them, do you?"

"I don't care. I'm gonna shoot them anyway."

"In that case, it's a good thing you don't have a gun, isn't it," she glared at me. "And even if you did, you wouldn't be shooting any cats."

With a heavy heart I left the house, picked up my traps and started walking back to the trapline. Today I had two squirrels less than I had yesterday. I was back to zero.

I reset the two traps that had produced the big results yesterday and checked the rest. There were no more squirrels. It was a hopeless situation. Yesterday I could just feel those soft genuine Indian moccasins on my feet; today they seemed so far away.

The week dragged on as I thought about those two lost squirrels, and the cats were avoiding me like the plague. They knew that to get too close was to risk getting the toe of my boot.

Saturday produced another squirrel and things started

to look up. I rigged up an old bird cage and hung it in the woodshed so that the cats couldn't get at my prize. Here I would store the squirrels until Dad came home.

By the time Christmas arrived, I had a dozen squirrels and one weasel. Once again I could just feel those genuine Indian moccasins. Dad came home and the first thing I wanted him to do was to skin and stretch my fur.

"Look at this, Dad," I beamed as I carted the bird cage into the house and shook the contents out onto the kitchen floor. The little frozen carcasses clunked on the linoleum like chunks of ice.

"Well lookie here!" he said looking down at the mess laying on the floor. "You done real good."

I stood there just popping the buttons off my shirt, I was so proud of myself.

"We'll get to them later," he said. "You better put them back in the shed for now." It seemed as though Dad had other things to do and my pelts were not his number one priority.

I stood there totally deflated. What could be more important than skinning my squirrels and the best of all, the weasel, I wondered as I slowly picked up the little animals and put them back in the cage one at a time.

Every time I walked into the woodshed, I'd stand there and look at the birdcage with the squirrels crammed inside. The weasel's fur was snow white with just a tinge of yellow, it's tail tipped a jet black. It really stood out against the brown and reddish hues of the squirrels. But it mattered not, they were never going to get skinned. No one seemed to care whether or not I got a pair of genuine Indian moccasins.

"I think maybe it's time we got around to skinning those squirrels," Dad said as if it were no big deal.

I charged out of the house, into the woodshed, grabbed the birdcage and roared back into the house. The weight of the world had been lifted from my shoulders. I was ecstatic as I dumped the frozen bodies on the table.

"Hold on now," yelled Mom. "Not on my table." And with a spoon she proceeded to flick them onto the floor.

I watched in horror as one by one she flipped them off the table. Thunk. Thunk. They crashed onto the floor, bounced, then skidded across the room. There were frozen squirrels scattered all over the kitchen by the time she finished.

"If I ever catch you pulling a stunt like that again, young man, those squirrels will stay in the woodshed. Do you understand?" she warned me.

I had certainly succeeded in getting Mom's attention. I guessed that she didn't really like squirrels that much.

"Okay Bob, pick them up and bring them over here by the fire to thaw out," Dad said calmly as if nothing had happened. "We'll skin them tonight. They have to do some thawing first. In the meantime we'll have to build us some stretchers."

The rest of the afternoon was spent building enough stretchers to hold each pelt. By the time we were finished, the squirrels had thawed and the skinning began. Dad did all the skinning and then he showed me how to pull the hide onto the stretcher. "Always put the fur on the inside," he instructed, "so that the pelt doesn't stick to the board."

"When can I sell them?" I asked, eager to get into town and get the genuine Indian moccasins.

"They have to dry first," he said. "Maybe in a couple of weeks. You'll be able to tell when they're dry. The skin will sound like dry paper when you ruffle it. Now don't take them off too soon or the pelts will shrink and you'll lose money when you sell them. We'll take them in and sell them when I come back from camp in the spring."

I continued to run my little trapline, but my focus was really on the stretchers and the drying pelts. Finally, the day I had been waiting for. The pelts were ready to be removed from the stretchers and we were going into town for the day. Dad wasn't home yet, but I couldn't wait to sell those pelts and get me those genuine Indian moccasins. I wrapped the pelts in brown paper and tucked them under my arm for the walk into town.

I was proud as a peacock when I strutted into that fur buyer's office with my pelts.

"Let's see what you got there, son," he greeted me as I walked through the door.

I strolled up to the counter and laid my package on the table. He grabbed the paper and tore it open, revealing twelve squirrels and one weasel pelt. I stood there beaming, looking at them like they were gold.

"Lemme see your licence, son," he asked without looking up.

"Licence?" I muttered.

"Yes son, your licence. I need to see it."

"I don't have a licence," I stammered.

"Well son," he said, leaning over the counter. "If you're gonna trap, ya need to have a licence." He was glaring across the counter at me. "And if you want to sell fur, ya need to have a licence."

Suddenly I was scared. It was getting hot and stuffy in there and I was starting to sweat. I looked at the door. I was ready to run.

"I can't buy these from you if you don't have a licence," he said, shaking his head sadly. He was feeling sorry for me, I thought, but not nearly as sorry as I was feeling for myself.

"I didn't know you needed a licence," I whispered. Suddenly I didn't feel like such a big shot. The counter seemed to have grown and I was having trouble looking over the top of it.

"Where'd you get these pelts from, boy?" He really sounded stern all of a sudden. "They don't look like they been handled by no kid."

"I trapped them on our farm," I whispered. "And my Dad helped me skin and stretch them."

"Oh," he smiled and straightened up, "trapped them on your own place, did you son? Well speak up, boy."

"Yes sir," I muttered again.

"Well now, that's different. But, you should have a licence, mind you. You could go to jail for trapping without a licence, you know." He was talking like a real friend now. "But don't worry, I'll take care of you. You just don't tell anyone, okay? It'll be our little secret."

Boy, this guy was suddenly my friend, and he was gonna help me out so I didn't have to go to jail. "I won't tell anyone. Honest," I blurted out.

"That's my boy," he said. "I could tell you were a good boy when you walked through that door. Now how much do you think these skins of yours are worth?" he asked, looking at the skins. He had a frown on his face as he tried to figure out their value.

"I was hoping to get enough to buy a pair of those genuine Indian moccasins there," I said, pointing to the moccasins behind the counter.

"The genuine Indian moccasins, eh," he said and scratched his chin as he carefully picked up each pelt and assessed it. He scribbled some numbers on a piece of paper. He stood there shaking his head as if the numbers didn't add up. "The way I figure it, son, them hides is worth less than them genuine Indian moccasins is."

He paused and pondered the situation, looking at the skins, then at the moccasins and back again. I was standing on pins and needles while he deliberated.

"You look like a pretty good kid, so I'll tell you what I'm gonna do. I'm gonna give you them moccasins for your hides. What's say we shake on it and we got a deal. How's that sound?" He was looking me right in the eye and smiling. He was a real nice man, I thought.

"That sounds great to me," I smiled, sticking my hand up on the counter. It was everything that I had been dreaming of. I was grinning from ear to ear as I watched him wrap the genuine Indian moccasins in brown paper.

"You got a pair of them ankle rubbers?" he asked.

"Yes sir," I replied.

"Well you always wear them moccasins inside a pair of those rubbers, it keeps them dry and they'll last longer," he instructed.

"Now remember, son, we don't tell anybody about them pelts or about our deal. I don't want everybody coming in here taking advantage of me the way you did," he cautioned.

I swore an oath of secrecy and headed for home. Man, but it was a great day.

By the time the rest of the family got home that evening, I was strutting around the house in my new genuine Indian moccasins.

I had been so pleased with them that I hadn't waited for the rest of the family. I had rushed home ahead. The first thing I did was to put those genuine Indian moccasins on my feet. Man, did they feel good, so good in fact that I rushed right out and did all my chores.

My chores were done. I could just sit around and enjoy

the fruits of my labour while everyone else tackled theirs.

Mom was not too pleased when she found out what had happened. "You should have waited for your father to come home," she stated angrily. "He told you he'd take you to town when he came home. That old bugger took advantage of you. If you had waited for your father you could have gotten enough money for those skins to buy five pairs of moccasins. Those damn fur dealers are all the same. They steal the poor trapper blind." Mom was pretty steamed up as she charged around the kitchen getting supper ready.

I didn't want five pair of moccasins, I only wanted one pair and they were on my feet. While everyone else was busy doing their chores, I sat around looking at my feet, admiring my new footwear.

The smell from the moccasins drifted into every room in the house and Mom made me take them off and leave them by the door with the rest of the outdoor footwear. I protested, arguing that they were meant to be worn indoors as well as outdoors, but Mom was adamant. She won out as usual. I think Mom was just upset about the fur dealer. I knew she'd get over it and by morning she would appreciate the rich aroma of the smoked genuine Indian moccasins.

When I went to bed that night, I could still smell smoked moose hide. The smell was throughout the house, there was no escaping it. In the morning I awoke, and the smell was still there, just as strong as it had been the night before. I jumped out of bed. I was in a hurry to do my chores. Of course I would be wearing my new genuine Indian moccasins.

"Mom," I screamed. "My moccasins are gone, somebody stole them. They're not here. I left them right here by the door last night and they're gone." I just knew that someone had snuck into our house last night and stolen them. I was heartbroken.

"They're out in the porch," Mom called out. "And they're going to stay there."

"Why?" I asked. "Why do they gotta stay in the porch? Everybody else's shoes stay inside."

"Because they smell, that's why. You've only had them one day and already everything in this house smells like moccasins. I'm not going to have my house smell like that all winter. If you want to wear them, you'll have to put them on outside and take them off out there. They're not coming back into this house."

"But it's cold out there," I whined.

"I guess you should have thought of that before you bought them."

Every time I went outside on Sunday, I had to stand out in the cold and pull the genuine Indian moccasins on, then wrap them around my leg and tie them with the moose-hide lacings. Even if I couldn't bring them back into the house, they were great.

"I'm gonna wear my moccasins to school tomorrow," I told everybody at the supper table. I couldn't wait to show my friends.

"Oh no you're not," Mom stated quite emphatically. "Those moccasins are going to stay right here on this farm. They're not going to go to any school, worn or otherwise."

"But Mom," I protested, "I just wanna show them to my friends."

"No! Now that's final. I certainly don't want anyone to think that my house smells like those moccasins."

Mom watched me pretty close as I dressed and left for school the next two mornings, but on Wednesday I was able to sneak into the porch and get the genuine Indian moccasins.

All the way to school I thought of the best way to surprise my friends. After carefully considering all my options, I reached a decision. I wouldn't take my rubbers off in the cloakroom. I would leave them on until I got into the classroom and was seated at my desk.

Once class started, I would secretly pull the rubbers off and casually slide my feet out into the aisles. One foot in each aisle, that way more kids would see my genuine Indian moccasins.

I could just imagine the boys all standing around admiring my genuine Indian moccasins and the girls asking if they could smell them again.

I arrived at school just as the bell sounded. I was so excited I could hardly wait to show everyone my genuine Indian moccasins.

I entered the school, walking through the west side doors and started up the steps, two at a time, heading for the grade four classroom. About halfway up the steps, I could detect the distinct odour of smoked moose hide.

"You smell something?" I heard someone behind me ask.

I was gonna turn around and say "That's my genuine Indian moccasins," when another voice said, "Yeah, it stinks like hell in here today."

"What is it?" asked the first voice.

"Beats me," replied the second voice. "But it sure stinks in here today. This is the worst that it's ever smelled in this school. Maybe the janitor shit himself."

They both laughed. I gained the top of the steps and headed for the cloakroom.

Suddenly I wasn't so sure that I wanted anyone to know what I was wearing. I quickly put my coat on a hook in the cloakroom and raced to my desk where I sat down and didn't move for fear that someone would notice my feet.

The smoked moose hide aroma followed me in, but it didn't stay there. It was drifting rapidly throughout the red brick schoolhouse. The smell was just as strong in one room as it was in the other. It showed no preference as it invaded the whole school.

Margaret, the little snit, sat in the desk right in front of me. I thought she had been obnoxious in grade two, but that was nothing compared to what she was in grade four.

"Oooohhh, do you smell that awful smell?" She turned around and wrinkled her nose like she had been poisoned. "It's just everywhere in the school. I think it's just terrible."

"I don't smell anything," I said, burying my head in my book trying to ignore her. But Margaret wasn't the type to be ignored.

"Can't you smell it, Bobby Adams?" she scolded me. "Doesn't your nose work?"

"I can smell something," I said to get her away from me. "But it's not that bad."

"If you can't smell that horrible stink then your nose doesn't work any better then your brain!" she snorted at me.

Margaret sure knew how to make a person feel good. She was so sensitive and considerate of other people's feelings.

My sister Gwen was in the same classroom. I glanced over at her. She was glaring back at me. She knew what the smell was. I tried to give her my best "if you tell I'll beat you up" look. Then I prayed that she would keep her mouth shut.

About a half-hour into the class, I had to go to the bathroom. I really didn't want to draw attention to myself, but the call of nature was too great. I raised my hand and didn't even have to ask for permission to leave the room.

The teacher immediately said, "You may leave the room, Bobby." I noticed that on this day the teacher didn't hesitate to give anyone permission to go to the bathroom. There was a steady parade of kids leaving the room all morning.

I bolted from the room and ran down the stairs to the basement where the washrooms were located. The washrooms always smelled like disinfectant, but not today. As I charged through the door I was greeted by the smell of genuine Indian moccasins. Oh no, I thought, the smell is everywhere.

For the rest of the morning, I sat there at my desk with my feet planted firmly on the floor and my pants pulled down as far as they would go, covering my genuine Indian moccasins. I didn't move a muscle until lunch time when the teacher made us all go outside to play.

"It's too nice a day to stay inside," she said. "A bit of fresh air will do everybody some good."

The principal, the vice-principal and the janitor, the three people in the school I feared the most, and a number of teachers were gathered in the hallway. "Seems to be in every room," the janitor was saying. "I haven't been able to pinpoint it yet, but I will."

Now I had everybody searching for my genuine Indian moccasins, I thought as I rushed for the door and the safety of the outdoors.

Outside in the fresh air, my fears soon vanished along with the smell. I was enjoying the day for the first time since I walked through the school doors. At last, I could enjoy my genuine Indian moccasins.

It was nice to see how well my moccasins performed in the snow. I raced into the deeper snow that others shunned because they didn't have adequate footwear. By the time the bell sounded calling us all back into school, I had succeeded in getting quite wet. I had even forgot about the smell that had engulfed the school house. But not for long.

As I walked towards the door, my brother walked up beside me. "Mom told you not to wear those stinky moccasins to school."

"Don't you tell," I snapped, "or I'll beat you up."

"I'm gonna tell Mom. You stunk up the whole school this morning."

I noticed that the genuine Indian moccasin smell had not diminished at all over the lunch hour. In fact, I thought that it might have got a little stronger. I raced to my desk and planted my feet on the floor again, determined not to move. Gwen was really glaring at me now.

"Ooohhh, that horrible smell is still here," whined Margaret. "Can't you smell it yet?" She turned on me.

"Yeah, I can smell it a little now," I mumbled.

"I feel like I could be sick to my stomach," she moaned.

As soon as the snow on my pants and moccasins started to melt, the smell definitely got stronger. My feet were right under my desk and I could almost feel the fumes as they rose from my damp footwear.

There was no doubt the smell was getting much stronger. I could hardly stand it myself. I had to do something about the location of my feet. The smell was no longer a pleasant odour. It had become a stench and I was getting it all. I had to share my experience with someone else. Prissy little Margaret was perfect.

I slid my feet forward, being careful that my pant legs did not pull up. They came to rest under Margaret's desk.

The warm moist fumes were now curling up under Margaret. I could just picture them raising up under her seat along her dress. Into her nose they would go and choke her.

"Something stinks in here," Margaret suddenly yelled and jumped from her desk. "I'm going to be sick to my stomach." She retched like she was gonna puke right on the floor.

Margaret's sudden reaction scared the dickens out of me and I quickly pulled my feet back from under her desk as the teacher came running to her assistance and led her from the room. I sweat bullets the rest of the day, waiting until school was out. Anything could have gone wrong. Gwen or Larry might just snitch on me. The janitor might catch me. There were a lot of things that could go wrong. I was sure that I wouldn't live the day if anybody discovered that my genuine Indian Moccasins were the cause of all the commotion in the school. When the bell rang at the end of the day, I wasted no time in putting distance between me and the schoolhouse.

At home, I hung the moccasins in the porch and went into the house. Suddenly the house took on the enhanced smell of the damp genuine Indian moccasins. There was just no hiding from it.

"Have you got those moccasins on in the house again?" Mom yelled threateningly at me as she charged into the room and stared at my feet.

"No Mom, I haven't brought them in the house since you told me not to."

"Then how come they're smelling my house up again?" she demanded.

"I don't know," I replied. "I didn't wear them in the house. I took them off in the porch like you told me."

"Robert wore them stinky things to school today and they stunk up the whole school," my sister snarled, as if she had been waiting all day to get me.

"Tattletale," I yelled at her.

"Didn't I warn you not to wear them stinky things to school?" Mom growled at me.

"Yes."

"I think it's time you did your chores," she snapped. "I'll have to see about those moccasins."

When I finished my chores and went into the house for the night, I hung my genuine Indian moccasins on a nail in the porch.

The next morning I went out to the porch to put my genuine Indian moccasins on to do the chores.

"Mom," I yelled. "Someone's stolen my moccasins. They're gone. They're not in the porch."

"I don't think anybody stole them," Mom replied calmly.

I looked at her questioningly. It seemed to me that she and those damn cats had the same guilty smirk on their faces.

DOUBLE-CLUTCH

My father, Bob Adams, had to be the most patient man in the world. It mattered not if he was standing waiting for a small child swinging a big hammer trying desperately to pound an elusive nail into a board or painstakingly trying to teach my mother, Florence, to drive a car. He never chided them, never growled at them to hurry up. He never raised his voice. He would coach and encourage them, waiting for as long as it took. That they were trying was the important thing, not how quickly they would master the task.

I fondly recall Dad's patience the summer I helped him build the gate leading into our yard.

It was destined to be the best gate on the south road. There was not another like it to be found anywhere in our area and my dad was building it. It would match perfectly with the rail fence that separated our house and garden plot from the rest of the property.

"How come these posts are so long?" I asked as we stood looking at peeled pine poles about twenty feet long.

"They're the gate posts. We're going to put them about

four feet in the ground," Dad replied. "Once we get them set into the ground they're going to have a cross beam on the top of them. They have to be tall enough for a loaded truck to get under that cross beam."

"Wow," I said, looking at the length of the posts. "How are we going to get that beam up there?"

"That's no problem. We'll nail the cross beam on while the poles are still on the ground and then we'll raise them."

With that, Dad set about measuring the exact distance he wanted the two main poles to be apart and the right spots to place them on both sides of the driveway. At each location, he drove a small peg in the ground.

"Okay. If you'd like, you can start to dig the first hole right here," Dad said, as he handed me the auger.

I jumped to the task eager to help in the construction of the best gate ever. The auger was as tall as I and was a heavy cumbersome thing. I was determined. I gritted my teeth as I placed the biting edge at the spot where the peg was driven into the ground. I started to have trouble immediately. The auger was too long and I couldn't get enough leverage to start the hole. But I wasn't giving up.

"How you doing?" Dad asked, watching my futile attempt to move earth.

"Okay," I said as I grunted and groaned, working up a good sweat trying to get the biting edge of the auger into the surface.

"Would you like me to give you a hand?" he offered.

"I can do it," I said, getting a little hot under the collar. More determined than ever, I attempted to turn the cutting edge. No luck.

"Maybe if I had a go at it I could get it started for you. The first cut is usually pretty tough," Dad said.

Reluctantly, I stepped back and he took the handle and

turned it effortlessly into the soft earth. I watched as he bore the hole down about a foot. After two or three turns of the handle he would lift the auger out of the hole, removing a small amount of dirt each time and dumping it by the side of the hole.

When the hole was down about a foot and the auger handle no longer level with my eyes, he stepped back. "There. See if that's any better."

"Oh yeah, that's better," I said. Now I was able to get on top of the auger handle and turn it. I could feel the blades cutting into the soft black soil. I twisted and turned on the handle until I buried the blades completely. I was going to take out a big bunch of dirt at a time, not just a little bit like Dad had done.

Once I was satisfied that I had an auger full of dirt I reached down and grabbed the shaft close to the ground and then pulled upward to get the dirt out of the hole. Just like Dad, only I got more dirt in the auger. I congratulated myself as I tugged upward. But the auger didn't move. I pulled again, this time much harder. It still didn't move. I got both my feet over the hole, straddling it and heaved with all my might. Nothing. Now I was sweating and getting a little hot again.

"This stupid thing won't come out of the ground," I grumbled at Dad.

"What's the matter?" he said, walking over to take a look. He peered into the hole, along the handle, to where it disappeared into the dirt. "I think maybe you've bitten off a little more than you can chew," he said matter-of-factly and walked over and lifted the auger and all the dirt out of the hole. He deposited it on the pile. "It's much easier if you just take a small amount of dirt. Don't try to take the whole thing out at one time."

I picked up the auger and again lowered it into the hole. This time I was much smarter. I only took a small amount of dirt and was able to lift it out quite easily, just like I had seen Dad do earlier.

I dropped the auger back in and out came another cupful of dirt. Hey, I thought to myself, this I can handle. It's a snap. After taking about a dozen withdrawals of soft black dirt, I encountered some resistance down there and the auger was getting awfully hard to turn again.

"This stupid thing won't turn when it's this deep," I snapped and kicked at the handle.

Dad laughed. "Looks like you've hit the clay. Here, let me finish it."

This time I didn't argue. Dad finished all the holes that were needed. Then he measured the distance between the holes and cut the main beam for the top of the gate the same length.

"Now you measure the width of the top of each pole," Dad instructed. "When you've done that, then you have to measure the same distance back on each end of the main beam and mark them at that place."

"What for?"

"When you get that done, we're going to notch each end of the beam and spike it onto the long posts. So the sooner you get started, the sooner we can get this gate up."

"Can I hammer in the spikes?" I liked to pound nails, that was a lot easier than digging post holes.

"We'll see."

I did just as Dad instructed and before long we were ready to begin spiking the beam and poles together. I had my own hammer and when Dad said okay, we both started to pound away. He was on one end of the beam, I was on the other.

Tap, tap, tap, tap I hammered away at the first spike. I wasn't making much headway. Tap, tap, tap. At the other end of the beam I heard BANG, BANG, BANG and looking up I noticed that Dad had driven in three spikes and was coming down to see how I was doing. Tap, tap, tap my little hammer pinged. I had one spike about a third of the way in and another was bent from being hit on the side. "Looks like it was a little windy when you were working on that one," he said and laughed. Man, my father was patient. He just stood there and offered encouragement until I had finished. I'm sure that he could have finished the gate in the time it took me to pound those spikes in.

Finally, it was time to raise the posts and drop them in the holes. For this we needed some help. Dad got my Grandfather and an uncle to come over to help us. With their muscle and Grandfather directing and hollering encouragement, the posts were soon standing upright. I got to help shovel dirt into the holes and Dad tamped the dirt until each pole was standing straight and was firmly planted.

This was the frame for the gate. The peeled logs shining white in the sun looked absolutely beautiful. Looking at the house in the background through the gate was just like looking through a picture frame.

"This is only part of the job," Dad said. "Time to build the gate now. Let's go, time's a wasting."

With those words, we commenced to build a gate using the same type of peeled pine poles that had been used for the posts and beam. Dad carefully measured the distance between the posts and then cut four pine logs that were about a foot shorter than the opening. Two more pine logs were cut about three-and-a-half feet long. Each of these were notched like the main beam and the four logs were nailed into them. This rectangle of logs was the gate.

Dad had metal hinge brackets for just such a purpose and he set about attaching them to one end of the gate and to one of the upright poles. Once this was done, we hoisted the gate up and attached the hinges together. The gate was now hanging right where it belonged and would swing freely either way. Then a hole was drilled right through the poles at the opposite end. Dad had a long metal spike that he pushed through one end of the post and into the gate. This held the gate firmly in place. Man, was that a sharp-looking gate. Everyone else on our road had a wire gate. We had a real pole gate and bragging rights.

With the task of gate-building behind us Dad continued with Mom's driving lessons. It was difficult to tell whether or not she viewed driving the car as a necessity. She made many mistakes, but never seemed too concerned and laughed them off like it was all a big joke. Driving was not a serious matter with mother.

It was Sunday afternoon and time for another driving lesson. As Mom, Dad and the rest of the family piled into the car, I ran to open the great pole gate. I stood at the gate as the car jerked and jumped away from the house and came down the driveway.

RRRRR the motor would rev up and the car would jump. Stop. Jump. Stop, then stall. This process was repeated several times, before the car reached me and passed through the gate. It turned onto the south road where it stalled once again.

I closed the gate and got into the back seat with my siblings. Mom started the car again. Dad was sitting beside her in the passenger's seat giving instructions. "Now Florence," he said very patiently, "step on the gas slowly and let the clutch out at the same time and the car will move forward."

"Okay," Mom laughed. "I think I've got it now."

RRRRR the motor revved up again and she yanked her foot off the clutch like she had just stepped on a nail. The car jumped and shot forward like something had plowed into the back end, then stalled. Mom laughed again and the process was repeated.

Down the south road we travelled in spurts, the car jerking, jumping and stalling. Past Grandfather's place. Past Nick the Dog Man's Place. Through the gully. Mom herded the car all the way to the railway tracks. Here Dad got behind the wheel and turned the car around. Then Mom took over and the car lurched forward once more and started back down the south road. Suddenly, and quite unexpectedly, we were moving. Mom was actually driving and we all stood up behind the front seat to watch the road disappear beneath the front of the car.

As we passed Grandfather's place, Dad began to give Mom instruction for slowing down. "Now remember, Florence, you have to 'double-clutch' when you want to gear down," Dad instructed. "Take it slow and watch the road. Stay over on your own side. That's it."

"What do you mean 'double-clutch'?" Mom asked casually, as she guided the old car along like she owned the road.

If Dad had explained 'double-clutch' once to Mom he had explained it a hundred times. But he had the patience of Job. Each time he would tell her she had to 'double-clutch', she would ask what he meant by 'double-clutch' and then he would carefully explain the procedure again.

"When you want to either slow down or to get more power, you have to put the transmission into a lower gear. To do that, you step on the clutch and take the car out of gear, then release the clutch and step on the gas to speed the transmission up. Then step on the clutch again and shift into a lower gear and let the clutch out again," he would say without ever raising his voice or sounding discouraged. "That is called double-clutching."

"Okay," Mom would answer.

On down the road we would go with Dad offering instructions and Mom trying to follow them or if the mood hit her just right, she simply ignored them. When she got them right, Dad would praise her and when she didn't, he would start all over again.

All us kids were still standing in the back seat watching Mom, not saying anything while the car ate up the road on one side, as it headed for the ditch only to be rescued by Mom before it got there and then headed for the ditch on the other side. Mom certainly drove like the road was her personal domain. Dad just sat beside her in the passenger's seat calmly giving instruction and encouragement.

As we neared our driveway, Dad calmly said, "Now, double-clutch and slow the car down before we get to the driveway."

"What do you mean 'double-clutch'?" Mom asked, as if she had never heard the term before. She pulled the car way over to the left side of the road in preparation for turning right into the driveway. It was always better to take the driveway head on, that way there was less chance of hitting the ditch. When Mom got the car over to the left side of the road there was the immediate danger of the car plowing into the left-hand ditch. She wanted to make sure that when she turned right into the driveway she was going straight in. Mom didn't like angle shots at the driveway.

"It would be better if you stopped on the road before we get to the driveway," Dad told Mom, who was busy concentrating on keeping the car on the road.

We were approaching the driveway and Mom appeared to be giving all of her attention to staying out of the ditch. But this was one of the occasions when she chose to ignore Dad. She was laughing and enjoying herself, paying no attention to Dad's instructions.

"Double-clutch and slow the car down," Dad spoke again, but the car continued its path on the lip of the ditch.

The car arrived alongside the driveway and without warning, Mom cranked the wheels to the right and suddenly we were heading straight at the driveway and the gate which I had securely bolted with the metal pin.

"Double-clutch," yelled Dad, which surprised us, for he had suddenly lost his calm. "Double-clutch," he yelled again. We could all see the beautiful new gate with the shiny white peeled pine poles looming in front of us.

"What do you mean 'double-clutch'?" asked Mom again, quite calmly.

"Hit the brakes!" Dad screamed as the gate neared. "Hit the brakes!"

"Why?" asked Mom, unconcerned.

"STOP THE CAR! STOP THE BLOODY CAR!" Dad roared, as the front end of the car plowed through the only gate of its kind on the south road. We could all hear the cracking and snapping of timber as the poles bent and then snapped, giving way to the power of the automobile.

As if she suddenly realized what Dad had screamed, Mom slammed the brakes to the floor boards. This sudden and unexpected turn of events caught us all off guard. Still standing up behind the front seat, we were suddenly propelled forward. The sight of me flying through the windshield flashed through my mind as the car ground to a halt.

We were all stunned as we collected ourselves. Dad sat there for a second in complete silence.

Mom got out of the car as if nothing had happened. She turned and looked at Dad, then calmly stated, "If you wanted me to stop, why didn't you just say so? You didn't have to yell."

The rest of us got out of the car and walked back towards the mess of broken pine poles for a final look at what had been the only gate of its kind on the south road.

HERE BOY, LET ME HELP YOU

"Giddyup. Haaa. Come on, you stupid horse. Giddyup," I yelled, slapping the reins across the flanks of the bay mare.

There was no movement. She stood there like a ruddy statue, with her head hanging down, refusing to budge. In fact, she hardly twitched when I swatted her again.

I was cleaning the barn and had the mare hitched to the stone-boat. The stone-boat is a flat deck made of two-inch by eight-inch planks about four feet long and nailed to skids. At the front of the stone-boat on each skid was a large eye hook that had a chain strung between them. The single tree on the harness was hooked to the chain.

I had worked about half way down the barn cleaning the manure and straw from each stall. The stone-boat was loaded and had to be taken to the field to be emptied. For some reason, the dumb horse was refusing to move another step.

I dropped the reins and walked around to the front. Patting her on the neck I talked to her like I had seen Dad do. "Okay old girl," I encouraged her. "Let's go now." I took hold of the bridle and tried to lead her. She lifted her nose a couple of inches, but held firm.

No dice. That stupid animal just stood there. "Haaa," I yelled and yanked on the bridle. Her head lifted slightly with my tugging, but the rest of her stayed right where it was.

"C'mon you stupid horse," I yelled again and swatted her on the rear end. My best efforts were proving futile. She refused to pull the stone-boat out of the barn so that I could unload it and return to clean the rest of the barn. Try as I may, that mare would not budge.

"Yo horse. Giddyup," I yelled again, giving that stupid animal one more chance. Still no action. I was starting to get steamed as I stormed out of the barn.

I'll fix that stupid horse, I thought, as I picked up a length of two-by-four and started back into the barn.

"Hey, boy," a cheerful voice called out to me. "You got a problem with that old mare?" It was Grandfather. He came striding into the barn behind me. He had a big grin on his face.

"Yeah. I gotta clean this dumb ole barn and this stupid horse won't move. I've tried everything, but she still just stands there like a dummy. I'll be in here for the rest of my life with this old nag."

Grandfather just laughed. "You have to learn to talk the horse's language if you want them to work for you, boy," he chuckled. "Here boy, let me help you," He winked at me. "I've got a way with animals."

Grandfather took the reins in his hands, and very gently urged the horse on. "Come on girl," he cooed in a nice soft voice. "Giddyup now," and he gently tapped the reins on her rump.

There was barely a quiver on her rump where the reins

fell. That horse was not to be sweet-talked, by Grandfather or anybody else. She held firm.

"C'mon now," Grandfather raised his voice a notch. "Let's get a move on, girl. C'mon now, giddyup," he shouted and slapped the reins a good one. Still no action. It looked suspiciously like that mare was never going to budge.

Dropping the reins, Grandfather stormed past the stone-boat and up alongside of the horse, where he patted her neck and urged her to move forward. "C'mon girl," he barked. I never saw Dad raise his voice like that when he was trying to sweet-talk a horse. But then, Grandfather was never known for his patience. He snatched at the bridle and tried to lead the horse.

That old bay mare stood pat. Grandfather yanked on the bridle and hollered, "Giddyup now. Move it." Her head stretched out in front of her following the pull on the bridle every time Grandfather yanked the reins, but her body refused to move.

"I think you got her head out further then I did," I informed Grandfather. My bringing this accomplishment to his attention didn't seem to impress him. He ignored me.

Now it was Grandfather who was getting steamed. He was not used to anybody or anything disobeying him. That old bay mare was certainly doing a good job of it, though.

"Haaa. Now, giddyup," he cursed and swatted the mare a real good one. The reins snapped loudly as they slapped across her rear. That sudden outburst scared me and made me jump, but it didn't phase the mare. Her feet were planted firmly on the floor.

"Here, boy," Grandfather yelled at me. "Hold these reins for a minute," he growled as he slapped the leather into my hands and raced out of the barn. "I'll be right back," he threw the words over his shoulder.

Once again, I tried to urge the mare to move. Wouldn't it be great, I thought, if I could get her moving while Grandfather was gone. I'd be able to tell everyone that Grandfather couldn't get the mare to move, but I did.

"Giddyup," I yelled and slapped the reins. I was still slapping the reins and yelling when Grandfather returned.

"Okay. We'll see who's boss now," he chuckled. Grandfather had a devilish grin on his kisser and gave me a big wink.

He was carrying a bottle in one hand and a rag in the other as he walked over to the horse. "Stand back now, boy," he instructed me, "and don't hold those reins too tight. When she gets my message, she'll take off out of here like a bat out of hell. When she takes off, you drop them reins. You understand, boy? Just let her go."

Grandfather sounded pretty cocky. There was no doubt in his mind that the mare would be moving in short order.

"Now listen, boy, you watch me and remember what I say, you understand, boy?"

"Yes Sir," I replied, watching him closely.

"From now on, boy, whenever you want this mare to move you just yell these words. I guarantee she'll be moving." With that Grandfather poured some of the liquid from the bottle onto the cloth. He lifted the mare's tail and shouted "Giddyup horse," and in one swift motion took a swipe at her butt. Drops of liquid spurted out from the sopping rag as Grandfather plunged his hand in under her tail and with one fluid motion wiped downward.

That rag had barely touched that mare's butt when she suddenly got a couple of messages. Grandfather was serious and she had an uncontrollable desire to move. In fact, all hell broke loose. The mare whinnied and jumped straight up into the air. When she came down her feet were moving. That old bay mare was in high gear instantly. She was heading for parts unknown.

She took about four jumps. Each time she bounced, the stone-boat jerked and left a pile of manure on the floor. With the stone-boat in tow, she made for the door. Grandfather had to be quick to get out of the way and avoid being hit by the stone-boat as it went whizzing past him.

I watched in horror. I realized that stone-boat wasn't made for speed. It wasn't towing that straight. It jerked to one side, hitting the wall of one of the stalls. It lurched and flew into the air from the impact, sending manure flying. That jolt didn't slow the old mare down one little bit and the stone-boat careened across the aisle and struck another stall, sending the remaining manure flying. On sped the mare, the stone-boat jerking and bouncing along behind. Out of the barn and down the lane galloped the old bay mare, past the manure pile, past the trees and into the field.

I stood there with my mouth wide open. "Holy cow!" I said to Grandfather. "Did you see that?" I looked around the barn to assess the damage. One stall was broken and there was manure everywhere. It was on the floor, in the stalls, on the walls, on the windows and on the ceiling.

"There you go, boy," Grandfather turned to me and smiled. "Anytime you need to get a horse movin', you just call on your ole grandfather."

"Cripes Grandfather, now there's shit all over everything. How am I ever going to clean this mess up?" I moaned, looking around the barn. "This place is a disaster area."

"That's your problem, boy. I just got the horse moving

for you. You don't expect that I'm gonna clean your barn too, do you?" he laughed.

There's no doubt that he got the horse moving, I thought. I'd never seen a horse move so fast. "I'll bet that old mare is still running. What do you think, Grandfather?" I asked, having almost forgot that I still needed the horse. "How am I gonna get her back?"

"She'll get tired and stop," he replied, unconcerned.

"How'll I get the manure off the walls and the ceilings?" I asked, looking around me again as we walked to the door.

"Just clean it off the floor for now, boy," he winked. "The rest will dry up and fall off sooner or later."

We reached the door and looked out into the field. The mare was standing at the far end with the stone-boat still attached to the harness. I thought she looked pretty alert after her wild dash from the barn. She stood facing the barn with her head up and her ears forward.

"Go get her and bring her back," Grandfather directed.

"But what if she won't come?" I asked.

"Oh, she'll come alright, boy. That turpentine can be a real persuader. Remember though, all you gotta yell is, 'Giddyup horse.' She'll bust a gut to get movin' for you."

Grandfather was right. After that, every time I said, 'giddyup horse' to that old bay mare, she stepped right smartly and obeyed every command. Well, every command but one. For some reason, I had a heck of a time trying to get her to stop. I think she sorta lost 'whoa' somewhere between the turpentine and the far end of the field. But she sure listened real good to 'giddyup horse.' I didn't even have to yell at her any more.

I had to admit, Grandfather sure did have a way with animals.

YOU AIN'T SO FAST, OLD MAN!

October 11th, 1948. A day that would be indelibly etched in my mind. One might go so far as to say that on this day, I was imprinted.

October 11th, 1948 was my tenth birthday. In my mind, on this day I became a man. As the saying goes, I was definitely 'feeling my oats.'

For the past few years, whenever Dad was away working, I was 'the man of the house.' I, like everyone else, had chores to do, but being 'the man of the house,' I usually did them at my will. But they were always done.

It mattered not that today was my birthday, there were chores that had to be done. They should have been done long before company arrived, but they weren't. Chores like filling the wood box and pulling fresh water from the well had been ignored.

I had been enjoying my day since I got up in the morning and certainly didn't want to ruin it by letting a little thing like the chores get in the way. There had been plenty of friendly reminders, but I had put them off.

It was the middle of the afternoon on this day, my day. Relatives and friends were gathered to help me celebrate. I was the centre of attention, the man of the hour, the cock of the walk. I was strutting around like I was the number one man on the farm, the king.

I couldn't count the number of times that both Mom and Dad had asked me to fill the woodbox. "Bob," I heard and looked up. Dad came outside where I was playing with my guests and asked once more, very politely I might add.

"Bob," he said again now that he had my attention. "The wood box is empty and has to be filled now so Mom can finish cooking your birthday supper." Dad was letting me know that I had delayed long enough. "This is your job and I expect you to see to it right away."

At that moment I was very busy being important and really couldn't be bothered with a little thing like wood for the wood box. It was probably just coincidence that we happened to be playing right beside a large pile of firewood that had been cut and thrown into the yard. This pile of wood was huge, being our winter's supply, and it was better than ten feet high. It would have been a very simple task to simply pick up an armful of wood and cart it into the house. This was too simple a solution for an important man like me, the man of the hour, 'the man of the house.'

I looked at Dad, who was standing on the porch waiting expectantly for me to comply with his request, then I sized up that woodpile. Dad's pretty slow, I thought, and I'm pretty darn fast and tough, too.

Right now, I'm having too much fun to bother with chores, I reasoned. I bet I could get to the top of that woodpile before Dad could take two steps. A vision of me nimbly scampering up the side of that woodpile like a mountain goat flashed through my head. At the top of the pile, I sat down tauntingly. Dad, being slow and methodical, struggled to get up that wood pile. As he scrambled and groped his way up, finally nearing the top, I gracefully bounded down the other side while he floundered and struggled to maintain his balance. I waited until he had just about fallen down the far side, then quick like a fox, I could see myself dashing around the woodshed. Dad plodded along behind desperately trying to catch me.

Armed with the knowledge of my speed and agility, I decided on the spur of the moment that if Dad wanted that wood box filled, he was going to have to catch me and make me fill it. I'll show my friends who's boss around this house, I thought, at the same time I'll impress them with my footwork.

"If you want that wood box filled, 'OLD MAN'," I really emphasized old man, "then you had better just jump to it and do it yourself," I informed him.

My friends couldn't believe their ears. They all stopped and looked at me as though I had lost my mind. Then they looked to Dad for his reaction. Not a word was spoken as the tension increased.

Dad and I stood there staring at each other for a minute, Dad not believing what he heard and me waiting to see what his next move would be. He stepped off the porch and started to walk in my direction. His steps were measured, he was in no rush.

Ha...just as I thought. He's too slow. "You ain't so fast, either, 'OLD MAN'," I shouted over my shoulder and swiftly skipped the few steps to the edge of the wood pile. I looked over my shoulder. Dad was still advancing.

I picked a large block of wood that was standing on end

at the bottom of the woodpile. It was here that I would launch myself towards the top of the pile. As nimble as a goat, I bounced to the top of the block and sprang forward, onto the pile of wood. I congratulated myself, it was exactly as I had imagined it.

My foot landed on the first piece, right where I aimed. While flying through the air, I had already picked out my next foothold and upon touching down I pushed off again, reaching for greater heights. Whoa, I thought as the spring disappeared from my leg on the first landing. The stupid block wasn't steady, it turned when my foot touched it, causing me to slip. I ended up back on the ground. I cast a quick glance over my shoulder. Dad was still coming and he didn't seem to be in any hurry.

With my superior agility, I regained my balance and once more started up the side of the pile. Every block that was stacked on the pile above the ground was loose. Every one I stepped on rolled or turned over. I was getting nowhere fast, my quick feet were really pumping now. Another quick check over my shoulder told me that danger was getting closer.

Another thought entered my head, darn, I should have tried climbing this dumb pile before I threw out my challenge. I never realized how difficult it was to climb onto a pile of firewood, especially when I was in a hurry. Suddenly, I realized that I had better get a move on. I was rapidly clawing and kicking my way up the side of the pile. Blocks of wood were turning in my hands and rolling out from under my feet, rolling down the side of the pile onto the ground. I was throwing up a lot of obstacles even if I wasn't gaining any height.

Dad was still walking and he was getting closer. He had

a very determined look on his face. But not me, my look had passed determined, it was now more like panic.

I started to scramble faster, more desperate then ever to reach the summit. The harder I tried the less co-operative the blocks became. There were blocks of wood flying in every direction.

My guests were all standing around watching 'the man of the house.' I was putting on a magnificent show. I was running for my life.

My feet were pumping like little pistons as I tried desperately to prevent my butt from being burned. My hands and arms were grasping in vain for that one block that would hold and allow me to escape, out of harm's way.

Dad reached the woodpile before I was a quarter of the way up. He reached up and grabbed me by the scruff of the neck and with one hand plucked me off the side of the woodpile. My speedy little legs and strong arms were now clawing thin air. There would be no freedom, no escape.

Man, I thought, is Dad ever strong, as I dangled from his grip. Then he flipped me over and onto his knee in one quick motion. I suddenly had a new appreciation for his strength. Then, right there, in front of my guests, Dad proceeded to show me why it would have been prudent to fill that wood box earlier in the day.

As soon as Dad finished delivering his lesson, I leapt up and grabbed the axe. I'm a pretty fast learner. I didn't need a second helping. I was splitting wood. I was carrying wood. I was a picture of obedience.

"That's enough for now," Mom said.

"I don't mind. I'll fill it right up to the top," I replied, stacking wood above the lip of the box.

I looked at my guests sitting around the table enjoying

fried chicken. What a birthday party, what a present I had received, the savvy and strength of Dad still stinging through. Certainly a day that I will never forget, I thought, standing at my place at the table. It was the only time my father ever spanked me. It was my tenth birthday. It was October 11, 1948.

WHAT'S THE MATTER, CHICKEN?

To say that I desperately wanted a .22 calibre rifle of my own, to hunt squirrels and grouse, would be an understatement.

"Why don't you just take up a hobby?" Mom would ask whenever I started talking about a .22. "It would be so much simpler."

Whenever I wanted to hunt, I had to walk to Grandfather's farm and borrow his .22. He never refused my requests, however this arrangement did have its shortcomings and nine out of ten planned hunting trips never succeeded in getting past Grandfather's farm.

The greatest danger to my hunting plans lay in Ma's kitchen. Ma was an excellent cook, and Grandfather would always suggest that Ma would be sad if her latest efforts were not sampled. If a batch of cookies was coming out of the oven when I arrived, she expected me to stay for cookies and hot chocolate. I would never think of disappointing Ma. I would force myself to stay, sample her cooking and render my decision on their degree of excellence.

Sampling Ma's cookies was never a simple matter. First,

those cookies already out of the oven had to be sampled while she made the hot chocolate. While the hot chocolate was being sipped, Ma would pop another batch of cookies into the oven and these too would have to be sampled. After an afternoon of eating and sipping, rarely was there enough time left to take the rifle, go hunting and return it to Grandfather before it got dark or worse, before it was time to do chores.

It was also possible for me to arrive and find that Grandfather wasn't home. This was a common occurrence. Then, of course, I couldn't get the rifle. When Grandfather wasn't home there was an excellent chance that Ma would be gone as well. Then my walk to his farm was really for nothing. Not only was there no rifle, there were no cookies, no hot chocolate.

It seemed like I was spending most of my time running up and down the south road to Grandfather's and very little of my time hunting.

Grandfather's .22 was only a single shot Cooey® and it was old, even by his standards. I had a love-hate relationship with that gun. I loved it because it was the only gun I had, but I hated to use it, because it was so old. It probably didn't shoot as straight as a new one would, either. I had my eye on a Cooey® bolt action repeater. It cost only $13. That was always about $12.75 more than I ever had in my pocket at any one time. The $13 and the Cooey® repeater were both something to dream about. Their chances of becoming realities were about as good as a snowball's chance in hell. Maybe someday, but for now I would have to settle for Grandfather's single shot Cooey®, whenever it was available.

When I first started using Grandfather's .22 I found the stock along the barrel far too large for my hands. The stock was the standard Cooey® design, heavy and bulky. I found it very difficult to hold and I often missed what I was shooting at. I told Grandfather. I told Mom and Dad. I told everyone who would listen that Grandfather's gun was too old and too bulky; not only that, it didn't shoot straight and that was why I needed my own gun.

Grandfather just laughed and said he couldn't do anything about the old part, but he could about the stock. One day I had run all the way down to his place to borrow the .22.

"It's not here," he said. "I took it to get the stock fixed for you. It'll be back in a couple of weeks."

Two weeks without a rifle. I wasn't sure I could make it that long. Once again I was thankful for Ma's cookies and hot chocolate. It wasn't a completely wasted trip.

I hounded Grandfather every day. I was going to make sure that as soon as that .22 was returned, I would have the first opportunity to use it.

Grandfather brought the .22 to our house the day he got it back. He didn't wait for me to come calling. It was laying on our kitchen table when I got up. I thought for sure I was looking at a new rifle. I looked at Grandfather who was sitting there grinning from ear to ear. "Well boy, what do you think of the old girl now?" He beamed like a proud father.

I stared at the gun in amazement. It was the most beautiful thing I had ever seen. Gone was the heavy hunk of battered wood that had been the stock. In its place was a sleek slim tapered stock that clung to the barrel like the two were one. The butt-end of the stock had been completely refinished. The entire stock had been coated with a warm glossy varnish. The light danced as it reflected off its polished surface. The barrel had been re-blued. It looked like a different rifle. It looked like a brand new rifle. I had never seen one like it before. It was the most beautiful thing I had ever laid my eyes on.

"Here boy," Grandfather said as he picked it up and handed it to me. "See if this old girl shoots any straighter now." He winked at Mom.

I reached over and took the rifle from him. "Wow!" I exclaimed as the smooth surface touched my fingers. Its finish felt even smoother than it looked. Slowly, I ran my hand down along the stock and the barrel. I marvelled at how I was able to wrap my hand completely around them both, my fingers touching over the top of the barrel.

I lifted it to my shoulder, the butt plate nestled perfectly in place. The stock felt like satin against my cheek as I looked down the barrel. The bead on the front sight dropped right into the V-notch on the rear sight. It was everything I had ever dreamed about. At that moment, the world was a perfect place.

"Well, boy. What do you think of that old gun now?" asked Grandfather, beaming like a Cheshire Cat.

"She's beautiful." I spoke softly as I ran my hands along the length of the stock. "She's so smooth. There's not even a little nick in her," I said, aiming it around the room at everything in sight. "I bet she'll shoot straight now. Can I borrow her and try her out?"

"Tell you what I'm gonna do," he said. "I'm gonna let you use that gun, boy, but just until you get one of your own. You can keep it right here with you. Now, how does that sound?"

I couldn't believe my ears. "That sounds great, thank you, thank you," I said, as I took off out the door. I had to try the new gun. Look out, tin cans! Look out, bottles! Look out, pine cones! Today they were all fair game. At least as long as the ammunition lasted.

I loved that rifle with the customized stock and marvelled at how light it felt in my hands, but like all things, the novelty of the sleeker, lighter .22 wore off. I had shot hundreds of shells and had mastered the little rifle. I could pick a pine cone off the very top of a pine tree. Instead of just trying to hit the squirrel I would pick its eye out. I shot grouse in the head instead of the body, preventing the wastage of meat. I was a budding Daniel Boone.

I started to yearn for bigger and better things. My dreams turned to Dad's big game rifle. More and more I would find myself standing in front of Dad's closet admiring his hunting rifle. It was an old 45-70 Model 1870 Winchester®. It was just like the ones I would see on the old Western movies at the theatre on Saturday afternoons. It was a marvellous piece of work and although it was old, it had character. I wanted to shoot that gun so bad I could taste it.

The 45-70, like the .22, was a single shot rifle. The breach broke to the top lifting up and the large cartridge would be dropped down and then pushed forward by hand. There was a large hammer at the side of the breach that had to be pulled back three notches before it was cocked and ready to fire.

I wasn't allowed to touch that rifle, but I could tell just by looking at it that it was quite a bit longer and heavier than the .22. The stock ran all the way along the barrel almost to the tip. It had a ramrod at the end of the stock for cleaning the barrel.

How I admired that rifle and longed for the day when I would be allowed to shoot it. I could just hear Dad say, "We're getting a little low on meat, Bob. I think it's about time that you went out and shot us a deer. What do you think?" Then he would hand me his big game rifle and I would be off for the woods.

I wasn't told not to touch the rifle shells and I would often take one and look at it. "I bet that rifle kicks like a mule," I would say, as I mentally weighed the huge 405 grain bullet in my hand.

One afternoon, a friend was visiting and the two of us were alone at the house. We had played trucks in the pile of clay by the outhouse, shot some marbles and were playing cowboys and Indians when the topic of rifles came up.

"My Dad has a gun just like the U.S. Cavalry used to shoot Indians in the movies," I said.

"I betcha he hasn't," said my friend.

"He has too," I countered. "And it's really old and looks just like the ones in the movies."

"Yeah. Well, I betcha it doesn't."

"Oh yeah, well I can prove it to you."

"Betcha can't."

"Betcha I can."

"Can't."

"You wanna see it?" I asked. That was like asking him if he liked candy.

"Really!" he asked in amazement.

"Sure, I know where it is. C'mon." Away we went, off to Dad's bedroom and into his closet. I opened the door and moved away the clothes. There, leaning in the corner, was the old rifle.

"Wow!" he said, as he stood there looking, his mouth hanging and his eyes wide open.

"What's the matter," I laughed, "trying to catch flies with your mouth?"

"Holy cow!" he responded without taking his eyes off

the rifle.

"Ever see anything like that before?" I asked, feeling awfully important.

"Never."

"Would you like to hold it?"

"Do you mean it? Can I?"

I picked up the old rifle for the first time. Man, was it ever heavy, I thought, as I lifted it out of the closet. "Now this is a man's rifle, so you better be real careful," I said and handed it to him. He never said a word as he reached for it. Not realizing how heavy it really was he almost dropped it on the floor. "You gotta be careful," I scolded him. "That's a man's rifle you've got there. Not a toy. So you better hold on good," I said to him.

He held it for awhile, turning it over in his hands again and again, then raised it to his shoulder. He was having difficulty keeping the long heavy barrel steady as he aimed at an imaginary enemy. "Wow, it's just like in the olden days," he said. "Does your Dad ever let you shoot it?"

"Oh yeah," I crowed. "My dad lets me shoot it all the time," I lied. I wasn't going to let him think that I hadn't or couldn't.

"Betcha you haven't," he challenged. "This old gun would kick your head right off your shoulders."

"I have too."

"Prove it. Let's see you shoot it now. Betcha you're scared."

"Am not. Anyway my Dad says I can only shoot it when he's around. I'm not even supposed to handle it if he's not here. If he knew, he'd skin me alive."

"You're chicken. You never shot it. You probably don't even know how to load it."

"Do too," I said. "I'll show you." I went and got a shell

from the drawer. I returned with the shell in my hand and a sinking feeling in my stomach. Right now I was praying that Dad wouldn't find out that I was fooling around with that rifle. I wished I had kept my mouth shut. I wished we had never played cowboys and Indians. In fact, I wished my friend had never come over to my house in the first place.

"We better take it outside first," I cautioned. "Dad told me I should never have a loaded gun in the house."

Out on the front step of the log house, I opened the breach and dropped the monstrous shell in. It just lay there. I lowered the muzzle towards the ground and watched it slide forward into the chamber. Slowly I closed the breach and listened to it click into place. "There," I said, "nothing to it. Told you I could load it."

"Yeah, but you can't shoot it, though. You're chicken."

"I'll show you who's chicken. Put a can up on that fence post and I'll show you how to knock 'er off."

"Which post you want 'er on?"

"Put 'er on that gate post by the well," I replied, trying to put lots of authority in my voice.

Grabbing an empty can, he ran for the fence and set it on top of one of the gate posts and raced back.

My heart was really pounding. I was standing in the doorway and finally I was holding a real rifle, a man's rifle. The target had been placed and the bullet dropped into the chamber. I was about to graduate from kids' guns to men's rifles. I had dreamt of this moment for a long time.

Now I stood there wondering if it had been such a wise dream. I was scared to death that the bloody thing was going to kick my head off. I stood there holding the rifle and looking at the can. I knew I could have hit the can with the .22, but I wasn't so sure about the rifle. I was having a real struggle with myself. Should I get my head kicked off or put the rifle back and take the heat for being a coward and a liar?

This was not an easy decision. I stood there for a long time building my courage.

"You gonna shoot now or you still scared?"

"I'm just measuring the distance." I stalled for time and then slowly started to raise the gun. Suddenly the barrel seemed awfully heavy. "Holy cow," I thought, "I'll never get this thing to my shoulder. How am I ever going to hold it steady?" When the rifle finally came up to my shoulder, I pointed at the can. My heart was pounding like a trip hammer. I lowered the muzzle.

"What's the matter, chicken?" My friend goaded me.

"I have to lean against the door to get a better aim," I said, trying to think of a graceful way out of this. There was none. I backed into the doorway and leaning against the door jamb once more, raised the rifle to my shoulder. This helped steady the rifle, but did nothing for my nerves or the pounding of my heart. I pulled the hammer back. One click. Two clicks. Three clicks. It was ready to fire. I took careful aim at the can. I just knew I was gonna get kicked on my butt when I pulled the trigger. At that moment I was wishing I was more chicken than stupid. I closed my eyes and squeezed the trigger.

There was a tremendous explosion as the old 45-70 barked. My ears rang. I opened my eyes and to my surprise I was still standing in the doorway leaning up against the doorjamb. It hadn't kicked my head off, in fact, I hadn't even been knocked on my butt. I was shocked at how little the big heavy rifle actually kicked.

"You hit it!" yelled my friend excitedly. "You knocked that old can right off the top of the post."

"I know. I never miss with this rifle," I tooted

triumphantly. Like the big shot I was, I casually walked back into the house and returned the rifle to its proper place in Dad's closet. He'd never know it had been outside, let alone shot. I had proved enough for one day.

That can with a huge bullet hole in it lying beside the fence bothered me, but I waited for my friend to leave before venturing near it. As soon as he left, I went to retrieve that can. I knew I had better go and get rid of the evidence before Dad came home. He'd know for sure it was me that did it, because he never shot at tin cans. "A waste of good shells," he would say just before he tanned my hide for taking his rifle out.

The can was lying just behind the post. I picked it up to look at the hole. I was curious to know how close to the centre of the can I had come. There was no hole in the can. I looked around for a second can. There must have been one lying there all the time. No luck, I couldn't find a second one. I checked the can again. Maybe I had just grazed it, but there wasn't even the trace of a mark on it. I was trying to figure out how I knocked it off without hitting it. Then I noticed something else on the ground. Splinters. There were splinters of wood scattered all over hell's half acre behind that post. I looked back at the post. Now I was feeling sick to my stomach. "Holy Mackerel," I thought as I stared in disbelief at the backside of the post. Half of it was gone. Blown away. There was no way I could hide this from Dad.

I went around to the front side and looked at it. Sure enough, about two inches below the top of the post there was a pock mark about the size of a quarter where the bullet had entered. But it was nothing compared to the portion blasted out of the backside. As I surveyed the damage, I doubted there was enough left of the top of the post for the can to stand on anymore.

There was no way that I could ever try to hide that bullet hole. The fruits of my day of boasting were blasted into the gate post for all to see.

I went out of my way to be nowhere near that post when Dad was around. I knew that he had seen the damage, but had not said a word about it. Finally the day came when there was no avoiding it. Coming from the barn we had to pass through the gate together.

At the post, Dad stopped as if he were seeing something for the first time. He looked at the back of the post, the part that was noticeable by its absence. He shook his head. I died a thousand deaths.

He walked around to the front of the post and put his finger up to the quarter-sized pock mark. I sweated, waiting for the inevitable. Again he shook his head. "Close the gate," he said to me and walked on to the house.

Dad never said a word, but then he never had to. For me it was the worst thing that could happen. If he would only say something we could get it over with and get on with our lives. I could get on with my life. Every time he and I walked through that gate, he would stop and look, first at the part of the post that was no longer there, then at the pock mark. And every time he did, I would stand there with my head down, waiting for the hammer to fall. It never came.

I quit talking about the rifle and how I was ready for bigger and better things. That I was going to get my own .22 or to use Dad's rifle, I knew was not to be. What I didn't know then was that I had taken my first and last shot with Dad's 45-70.

TURN THEM LIGHTS ON, BOY

"Come on, girl. I haven't got all day." It was Grandfather's voice that woke me. I opened my eyes and listened.

"Are you sure you need them all?" Mom asked.

"Yes girl, I need all of Bob's guns and every shell as well," he shouted. "Come on, girl. Hurry up now."

Grandfather was pretty excited about something, I thought, as I jumped out of bed and pulled my trousers on. I raced to the kitchen where Grandfather was pacing back and forth. He wasn't his usual jovial self. He was concerned about something.

"What's the matter, Grandfather?" I asked, looking at his worried face.

"It's a bear, boy!" he said as he stopped pacing and looked at me. "It's a bear, I tell you. Biggest bear I ever seen. It got into my pigpen last night and killed one of my best sows. Just about got me, too." And he shook his head as if reliving the incident.

"Wow!" I said. "A bear. What happened?"

"Happened last night, after I'd gone to bed. Me and Ma

was sound asleep when the pigs started squealin' and the dog barkin'. Made such a noise, they woke me up. I thought it was that damn Chinaman. Thought he'd come back to steal another one of my pigs." He stopped and took a big slurp of coffee. "I got me out of bed and got dressed. I grabbed a flashlight and called to Trixie." Trixie was Grandfather's Fox Terrier dog. "When we walked outside, them pigs was really makin' a fuss, squealin' their fool heads off. I thought maybe that Chinaman had got himself into one of the sow's pens and she was workin' him over.

"The noise wasn't comin' from the barn, it was comin' from one of the side pens. I just jumped over the fence to see what all the fuss was about and shone the flashlight around. Hell, boy, I didn't know it was a bear." He stopped and took off his cap and wiped the sweat off his brow. Then he wiped the inside of his hat and returned it to his head.

"When I saw that bear in the light he was almost on top of me. I held that flashlight out in front of me as far as my arm would stretch." He stuck out his arm to show me. "That bear walked right up to the flashlight and had his nose almost on the end of it." Grandfather had to sit down before he could finish his story.

"I backed up, as far as I could go. I was right up against the fence. I couldn't go any farther and that bear kept comin' towards the light. I was so scared, boy, why I couldn't even yell for help." His voice had fallen to a whisper.

"Wow!" I replied again. I was thunderstruck.

"Then out of nowhere Trixie got into that pen with us. I don't know where he came from or how he got in there, but he did. I didn't think he could get into that pen. That little dog was barkin' up a storm, but that bear never paid him no mind at all. Suddenly Trixie got around behind the bear and he musta bit him." Grandfather's eyes got wide.

"That old bear let out a 'WOOF' and turned around to get at the dog. I saw my chance to escape," he said. "I cleared that fence in nothing flat and ran for the house." Grandfather sat there staring off into space. He was still pretty shaken by the whole experience.

"What happened to Trixie?" I asked.

"Well, I thought he was a goner," Grandfather replied. "When the ruckus died down, I called from the house, but he never came. He must have been chasin' that bear though, because when I got up this mornin' and left the house, there he was sittin' on the porch like nothin' had happened. Saved my life, he did. Best dog in the whole world." Grandfather smiled for the first time that morning. "Would you hurry up, girl," he called to Mom. She was in the bedroom getting Dad's guns and trying to find the ammunition.

"Are you gonna shoot the bear, Grandfather?" I asked.

"I sure am, boy," he replied, as if there was no doubt about it.

"Can I come too?" I pleaded. "I can shoot a rifle."

"I can use every man I can get," he replied. "I think I can use you alright."

"Oh boy, thanks, Grandfather," I warbled. I was as happy as a lark at the thought of hunting a bear with Grandfather. "I can use Dad's rifle!" Suddenly I could see the bear charging straight at me, snarling and roaring, his mouth wide open, his huge teeth gleaming. I stood my ground. Calmly I raised Dad's 45-70, took careful aim and fired. The bear dropped in his tracks. I was one cool cat in the face of danger.

"I don't think so," Mom intervened and brought my whole world crashing to the floor. Suddenly I was back in reality. Mom had come out of the bedroom carrying Dad's guns and two boxes of ammunition. "You'll be staying right here, young man," she said. "I'll have no more talk of you going bear hunting."

"He'll be okay," Grandfather spoke up. "I have a job for him. He'll be quite safe with me."

"I don't think that any part of bear hunting is safe and anyway he's a little too young to go bear hunting." Mom was standing firm.

"I'll be okay, Mom," I piped up. "I can handle Dad's rifle. I've shot it before," I blurted out without thinking. Dummy, I kicked myself. I had just made a terrible mistake. No one else in the house had mentioned the shot-up gate post. No one else, that is, until I opened my big mouth. I stopped and waited for the hammer to fall.

"I think that shooting up a gate post is quite a bit different than shooting at a real live bear," Mom countered.

That comment cut deep as the old memories flashed through my mind. I saw Dad once again stopping to look at the gate post and shaking his head. "Stupid! Stupid! Stupid!" I cursed myself. I looked to Grandfather and wondered if he knew about the gate post. How many people knew? If he hadn't known before, he certainly did now. I sat down dejectedly, feeling like a fool.

"I've got just the job for him," Grandfather said, breaking the silence. "That bear probably won't be back again until after dark tonight and we're going to be waiting for him. I'll need someone to turn the lights on so that I can see where to shoot. Now, I'd say that sounds pretty safe, wouldn't you, boy?" He looked at me and winked.

That didn't sound like a good deal to me at all. Not when I had visions of shooting a bear. Any girl could turn on the lights, I thought to myself.

"I don't think so," Mom responded. "I'm not crazy about having my son walking around with you or anyone else in the dark looking for a bear and who knows what. I think he'll stay right here in this house with me tonight, where it's nice and safe."

Mom sounded pretty darn tough and determined. The more I thought about my options, maybe turning on the lights for Grandfather wasn't such a bad idea after all. At least then I'd be close to the action, instead of sitting at home.

"He'll be fine," Grandfather said. "And we won't be walkin' around in the dark, girl. Len's goin' to help me. We plan to set up some lights that can be turned on when the bear appears. Len and I are goin' to be settin' up an ambush down by the barn."

"You and who?" Mom sputtered, as if she couldn't believe her ears.

"Len, the guy living in our bunkhouse. I talked to him already this morning. He's had lots of experience with bears. He said he'd be ready to help if I needed it."

"Don't tell me you're going to give that blowhard a gun?" she asked, as if she couldn't believe what she was hearing. Mom sat down, shocked. "Why, I wouldn't trust that man with a cap gun. The only thing he's ever shot is the 'bull'." Mom was quite emphatic in her dislike for Len.

Personally, I thought that Len would be the ideal person to help Grandfather. I had spent many hours listening to Len tell of the places he'd been and the things that he'd done. It seemed to me that he had been everywhere and done everything. His many stories about his hunting prowess were legend. The fact was, Len had shot many animals. Why, he even had a bear rug on the floor in front of his bed. What more proof would a person need? I agreed with Grandfather. Len was the perfect person to have standing beside you in a time of need.

"Len's okay," Grandfather defended him. "He knows how to handle a rifle and I need someone with me who can shoot straight. Don't worry about the boy. He'll be fine. I'll keep him with me."

"That's part of my concern," Mom replied, looking Grandfather in the eye. Mom was not impressed.

I was walking around the pigpen with Grandfather as he was formulating a plan of action. Mother had finally relented and I was now an official member of the bear team. I was following Grandfather around like a shadow and was in on every important decision.

The dead sow was still lying in the pen. "That's where she died, right where she lays," Grandfather said, as we looked at the carcass. Large pieces of skin and meat were torn from her back and neck. "She's our bait," Grandfather said. "When that bear comes back tonight for a feed of pork, he'll get a good surprise. Instead of a belly full of pig, he'll get a belly full of lead." We both laughed.

My role had been determined. I would turn on the lights. I looked around the pen. In my excitement I had forgotten there were no lights in the pen. In fact, there were no lights in the barn. I hadn't thought of that before. I'll bet Grandfather wants me to shoot after all. That crafty old fox, I thought. He just said that to trick Mom into letting me come. I was going to be shooting after all. My heart was racing as I looked around the pen for a good hiding place for me.

"I think we'll park the truck right over here," Grandfather said, as he pointed to a spot just in front of the pen.

"Looks like a good place to me," I agreed. Then,

thinking about it I asked, "What do you need the truck for, Grandfather?"

"That's where you're gonna sit, boy. When the bear shows up you're gonna turn on the lights so's I can shoot it," he replied matter-of-factly and once more my dreams of shooting a bear came crashing to earth.

"Where you gonna be?" I asked.

"I'm gonna be right over there beside the barn and Len will be over at that corner of the fence." He pointed out the two locations.

"How come I gotta be in the truck?" This was a real bummer, having to sit in the truck.

"Cause that's where the lights is, boy. You can't turn them on if you're not in there with them now, can you?"

"I guess not," I said dejectedly.

My disappointment did not last long and I was the first one of the bear team on the line. I had been there all afternoon, even though Grandfather had said it wasn't necessary to be out there until after supper. My job was only to turn on the lights, but I wasn't going to miss the bear for anything.

I had to be called to the house for supper. Then I had to be told to go to the house for supper. Reluctantly, I left my post. I gulped my supper down, not bothering to chew anything, and I hurried to get back to the truck.

"Here, take these with you," Ma said, as I started out the door. "It could be a long night." She handed me a thermos of hot chocolate and a bag of sandwiches. I grabbed them and ran back to the truck.

I sat at my post and watched as Grandfather and Len came down to the pen. They were each carrying an arm full of firearms.

Grandfather was setting up for his watch on my left,

right beside the barn. Len was on the other end of the pen to my right. I had the best seat in the house. I was in the truck behind them both and right in the middle. The excitement was mounting. I put my hand on the light switch and watched the pen.

Each of the men leaned their firearms against the fence right in front of them. Then they returned to the house and came back with more guns. There were guns of every description and calibre. There were rifles, shotguns and .22s. I could see Dad's 45-70 and his Bolt Action 12-gauge shotgun in front of Grandfather. Each man had about a dozen guns. That old bear didn't have a chance. I smiled as I tapped the light switch with my fingers.

Man, this was exciting, I thought, as I sat there looking at the two men, all the guns, the pigpen and the spruce trees beyond. "C'mon bear," I said to myself, "we're ready for you tonight." I watched as the sun slowly sank in the west and the dark shadows from the spruce trees lengthened over the pen, the two bear hunters and the truck. Then it was dark.

I sat there in the truck staring into darkness. Now sitting in a truck and staring into a pigpen in the daylight is nothing to write home about. But while it was light there was at least the chance of seeing the bear walk in. Now, sitting in the truck in the darkness, I couldn't see a thing and it was getting even less appealing. The excitement was waning as the time dragged on.

That ole bear probably won't show up anyway, I thought, as I took my hand off the light switch and poured myself a cup of hot chocolate and took out a sandwich. I was lost in the black of the night, alone with my thoughts, not even thinking about the bear. Thinking about nothing. Daydreaming. Just about to take the first sip of my hot chocolate.

Suddenly, there was a streak of flame that came from Len's corner of the fence. It shot across the front of the truck in the direction of the barn and was followed by a thunderous KABOOM.

That streak of fire and explosion scared me half to death. I jumped, my head snapped up and back and slammed into the back of the cab. My heart skipped a beat and leapt into my throat. The cup of hot chocolate flew from my hand, spilling its hot contents all over my pants and legs. "Yeow!" I yelled as the hot liquid burned my legs. I forgot about the bear. I forgot about the light switch. I frantically tried to brush hot chocolate from my pants.

At that very instant, somewhere in the distance, I thought I heard Grandfather scream out, "Aeeeyyyiiii."

Then there was another KABOOM. Then a loud bang. I heard something let out a terribly loud roaring bawl. Suddenly the night was filled with strange sounds and shots. Grandfather was yelling, "Turn them lights on, boy!"

I was busy frantically trying to get the hot chocolate off my trousers.

The shots continued. Grandfather was still yelling, "The lights, boy! The lights! For Christ's sake, boy, turn them lights on!" My legs were burning from the hot chocolate. I was trying to pull the cloth off my legs with one hand and fumble around for the light switch with the other.

Somewhere in the dark the light switch had disappeared. It had been right there, now it was lost, I thought, as my hand groped along the dash trying to find it.

Finally I found it and in my haste I turned it on, then off, then on again. As the headlights lit up the fence and part of the pigpen I could see Grandfather, without his cap on, standing up firing shot after shot into the darkness towards the side of the barn. When one gun was empty, he would set it down then grab the next and fire again. With each shot fire burst from the muzzle and streaked into the darkness towards the shadows.

On the other side of the pen Len was standing, staring in the direction of the barn. The shotgun he was holding was pointing into the air and he was having a devil of a time trying to work another shell into the chamber. Finally, he succeeded and fired another shot and a streak of flame burst from the shotgun heading towards the stars.

I peered into the darkness of the pigpen, but I couldn't see a thing. I certainly couldn't see any bear. Then from the direction of the house, I could hear Trixie, barking as he ran toward us. He dashed past the truck, through the fence and into the pigpen, darting into the shadows beside the barn. He disappeared and I could hear him growling and snarling.

Grandfather stopped shooting once the dog entered the pen. He stood there looking towards the noise. "Okay boy," he called to me, "you can come over here now."

"Did you get him, Grandfather?" I yelled as I jumped out of the truck. My pants were wet, my burning legs forgotten, as the excitement I felt earlier returned and I ran to Grandfather's side.

"There he is, boy," he said, pointing into the dark night.

"Where?" I asked, straining my eyes trying to see it. I could see nothing but dark shadows; the darkness of the bear was hidden in the night. "Are you sure there's a bear in there?" I asked as I leaned forward.

"There's a bear alright," Grandfather replied. "A very dead bear."

Grandfather forgot about the bear and so did I when he turned towards Len and roared, "What in hell were you shootin' at?"

Len was still over in his corner of the pen wrestling with the shotgun. He had not taken his eyes off the shadows beside the barn and it looked like he was still trying to get another shot away.

"Somethin's wrong with this damn gun," he complained. "You gave me a piece of crap to shoot and I can't get it workin."

"Well put it down before you shoot someone," Grandfather snarled at him. "There's nothin' wrong with the gun. You seem to have had it workin' well enough to have damn near shot me."

"I did not," Len snapped back, still working the action. "I got the first shot into the bear, then this gun went haywire on me."

"Put the gun down and come on over here, I want to show you something," Grandfather snarled again. "Look at this." He pointed to the pattern of buckshot on the barn above where he had been standing. "You shot the hat right off my head, you dummy."

"That wasn't me," Len protested. "I got the first shot into that bear."

"Well look around for Christ's sake." Grandfather was not a happy man right now. "There's only you and me here. Who else could have done it?"

"Not me," Len argued. "I emptied all my guns right into that bear. Anyway I'm not going to stand here and be insulted. I'm gonna take the guns back to the house."

"Don't you touch any of those guns," Grandfather ordered. "Bob here will take them back. At least he knows how to handle them."

My chest flew out as I walked over to the corner of the fence to pick up the guns. It was the first time that Grandfather had called me by my first name. I was now a grown-up.

As Len stormed off into the night, Grandfather yelled loud enough for half the country to hear. "Boy, you better just check the big game hunter's guns and see if he left any shells in them after he tried to kill me."

It didn't take long for Grandfather to forget my first name, I thought as he addressed me as boy at the first opportunity.

I picked up the first gun and pulled the bolt back. Out popped a live shell. I checked the next one. "These guns are all still loaded," I said to Grandfather.

"That's what I figured," Grandfather snorted in disgust. "The man of the world. The big game hunter panicked and damn near shot me. I tell you boy, I could have been killed."

I got busy and hauled the guns back to the house where Grandfather checked them all before stacking them in a corner.

We were all sitting around the table drinking coffee and hot chocolate, reliving the events of the hunt. I was sitting beside Grandfather as he described how that bear came walking through the spruce trees right up to the dead sow. He left out the part about Len shooting the cap off his head.

"I'm sure glad I had this boy here with me tonight." Grandfather smiled and slapped me on the back. "I couldn't have done it without him," he praised.

"As soon as Grandfather yelled for the lights, I turned them on so we could see the bear," I chimed in, wanting to make sure that everyone knew I had been included in this important event.

"Can we go see the bear?" one of the womenfolk asked.

"Not tonight," Grandfather said. "I think it's best we let him lay 'til mornin'. There'll be lots of time to look at him tomorrow. Anyway, it's too dark out there tonight."

"How big is he?" someone asked.

"What kind is he?" came another question.

Everyone looked to Grandfather for the answer.

"What colour was the bear?" someone asked me.

How big? What kind? What colour? Then it dawned on me. I never saw the bear. I never saw it when it walked in and I never saw it after it was shot. I didn't know the answers to those questions.

As I sat there in my wet pants, covered with cold hot chocolate, I bowed to a greater man. I, too, looked at Grandfather for the answers.

HE'S TOO STUPID TO BE DEAD

From the kitchen could be heard the clatter of dishes and cutlery and the humming of a Christmas carol. Mom was a happy caroller as she bustled around the kitchen cleaning up the dishes from a delicious supper. And what a supper it was; moose roast with mashed potatoes and gravy, mashed turnips, carrots and fresh home-made bread, home-made relish and dill pickles topped off with wild blueberry pie, made from blueberries that we had picked the previous fall and Mom had canned.

Dad was sitting in the living room tuning his guitar. Suddenly he started pickin' and singin'.

"Jingle bells, jingle bells, jingle all the way," Dad yodelled in his nasal country twang. We all joined in, my brother, two sisters and myself as we picked up the tune. I say picked up the tune loosely. My sisters sing like birds. Larry and I, on the other hand, should be out in a field where we can't scare anything. Our voices are terrible. I can't carry a tune to save my life. But it mattered little as we gathered around and joined in the festive spirit. We were all sitting on the floor at Dad's feet. We opened our little mouths and let the words ring forth.

It was Christmas Eve and as was the custom in our log house, after having eaten the feast that Mom prepared, she would clean up the kitchen, Dad would get out his guitar and we would sing our little heads off as he strummed and sang Christmas carols.

This was the evening to end all evenings. It was the one day that we waited for all year long. Dad would be home from the bush camp for the Christmas holidays. The whole family was together, there was laughter, music, song and plenty of food. It was the best of times, it was the greatest day of the year on the stump farm.

Dad could play any of the stringed instruments and when he did, we always had a great sing-song. There was no doubt about it, when Dad came home and the musical instruments came out, it was party time. He would play one or two songs on the guitar, then pick up the fiddle, the mandolin or the banjo. It mattered not, he played them all and each song would be sung to the accompaniment of a different instrument.

But Christmas Eve was special, it was the one night that we all looked forward to with great anticipation. First there would be the meal, then the clean-up and the singing of carols, which would get us all in the festive mood. Then it was off to Ma and Grandfather Ernst's house to await the arrival of Santa Claus.

Mom could be heard singing along with the group from the kitchen while she washed the dishes and cleaned up. Dad never stopped his strumming as we finished one carol and jumped right into the next. One after the other, we would go through each and every carol we knew. There was time enough for Dad to play each of them at least once and some of the more popular ones like Jingle Bells and Silent

Night would be sung two or three times.

"Okay. I'm just about finished," Mom would sing out. "It's time to get dressed now. We want to see if Santa comes and who's been good little boys and girls this year."

There was a flurry of activity as we all hustled to get into our winter clothes. Dad would head for the barn to get the horses and sleigh ready. Everyone was grabbing overshoes and pulling them on, reaching for parkas and toques and bumping into each other. Each was as angelic as they could possibly be. There was no pushing or shoving, no yelling "get out of my way," which would normally be heard when everyone tried to get dressed at the same time.

Yes, this was Christmas and Santa was coming. Everyone was on their best behaviour. Butter wouldn't melt in our mouths on this night. Once dressed, there was a mad rush for the door. Who would be first to get outside and wait for Dad to bring the horse and sleigh? Who would be the first on the sleigh?

Outside we dashed and stood in the dark silent night by the side of the log house. It was snowing, large soft flakes were drifting to earth. We waited silently for the sounds in the night that would tell us that the horses were harnessed and hitched to the sleigh. Suddenly we could hear the sleigh bells on the harness as the horses left the barn and came towards the house. We couldn't see them in the dark, but just hearing them sent shivers up and down the spine. Dad was on his way.

Christmas Eve was an exciting time and it was getting more exciting as each minute passed. Each minute brought Santa a little closer.

Around the side of the house came the horses and sleigh. We all cheered as the excitement mounted. "Whoa-up," Dad would call out as the sleigh came abreast of us.

"Whoa now." The horses were prancing and tugging at their bits. They too seemed to sense the importance of the evening. They were as excited as we were. "Okay Florence," Dad said to Mom. "You get in first, sit right here beside me. Now Judy," my youngest sister. "You sit right up front here between Mom and me. Larry, you climb up and sit here. Gwennie, you sit right there in the middle and Bob, you can sit beside your sister and hold my guitar."

"Just my luck," I mumbled to myself, "first one out the door and last one onto the sleigh." But, after all, this was Christmas Eve and we were off to see Santa. It was soon forgotten as I clutched the guitar.

Once Dad had us loaded into the sleigh, he would gently tap the anxious horses with the reins. Down the driveway they would prance, turn left onto the south road and head north to our grandparent's house which was a half-a-mile away.

"Mom, is Grandfather gonna be up when Santa comes this year?" I asked.

"I certainly hope so," she replied. "He certainly made a fool of himself last year, didn't he?"

"Yeah, he sure did," we all laughed.

But Dad cut our conversation short as the horses hit the road. He started to sing carols and we all sang along. The sound of sleigh bells ringing, everyone singing and large snow flakes falling made the evening feel like a magic moment in time. Truly it was the Christmas spirit. Everyone was in such a good mood and so happy it was, without a doubt, the greatest day of the year.

Ma was standing in the door when we arrived. "I could hear you coming," she smiled. "The sound of you singing Christmas carols was so beautiful." Ma was being very generous, I thought as I tried to imagine my tinny voice sounding beautiful.

"Has Santa been here yet?" someone yelled at Ma.

"He hasn't been here yet," she replied. We all cheered at the good news. "I heard on the radio that there are reports that he has left the North Pole, so he should be here before too long." We cheered again; the news was getting better.

"You had better come in here and get ready for him," she urged us. We ran for the door where Ma gave each of us a big hug and a kiss like we hadn't seen each other for years. Actually she saw us every day. We had to walk past Ma's house to get home from school and she would always call us in and give us cookies or cake. It irritated Mom, because she would say that it ruined our appetite and we wouldn't eat supper. But that didn't bother Ma one little bit. She would always just agree with Mom and then she would call us in again the next day.

"Grandfather's in the living room by the Christmas tree and he's already a bit tipsy," Ma huffed. "He's been into that filthy whiskey again and I'm not too happy with him right now."

Into the living room we charged and stood looking at Ma's Christmas tree. To me, Ma's Christmas tree was always the biggest and the most beautiful tree anywhere. Like most homes during these tough times, there were few presents under the tree. But that didn't matter because it was Santa Claus who brought the presents and he hadn't been there yet. The candles were already lit on the tree and the dancing flames rippled along the coloured angel hair. Fancy glass bulbs reflected light around the room. It was breathtaking.

"Merry Christmas everyone!" Grandfather shouted out as we stood around the tree. "Merry Christmas to you all."

I looked at Grandfather and knew immediately that Ma wasn't kidding when she said that he was a little tipsy. Grandfather was sitting in his chair close to the tree. He had a big old grin on his face as he greeted us. Then he started singing. He was in the festive mood, but he didn't know any Christmas songs. He burst into a rousing rendition of the only line of a song that I had ever heard him sing: "And under her belly I saw the blue sky." Grandfather was having a great time. He checked to see if Ma was looking. She wasn't and he quickly pulled his Mickey from his hip pocket and had a snort. It appeared that Grandfather was getting tipsier by the minute. Ma would not be pleased.

As the evening progressed other members of the family arrived. Aunts, uncles and cousins would drop in. The excitement continued to grow.

Some folks were singing carols, some looking out of the windows to see if they could spot Santa and his reindeer, others were picking out the best spots to sit around the Christmas tree.

Grandfather was enjoying himself. That funny grin never left his face. He stayed in his chair near the tree and watched Ma. As soon as she left the room, he would look around to make sure someone was watching. His face would light up, he'd throw whoever was watching a big wink, pull the Mickey out of his hip pocket and have another snort. His grin got wider each time Ma left the room.

Grandfather was getting happier and tipsier by the minute. Ma, on the other hand, was getting angrier. Soon most of us were watching Grandfather sneak another snort, then looking at the door where Ma had disappeared to see if she had caught him. It was a game in itself.

Suddenly Grandfather got so tipsy he toppled right out

of the chair and onto the floor. Head first he came, just missing the Christmas tree. He landed on his shoulder and lay in a heap. He didn't move a muscle, he lay very still, but he continued to wear that big stupid-looking grin on his face. Grandfather had passed out and Santa still hadn't arrived.

"Ma! Ma!" someone called out. "Grandfather's fallen on the floor. He's not moving." We all stood there wide-eyed with our mouths open as Ma came charging into the room. She looked at Grandfather, her hands on her hips. She was not too happy with Grandfather, who lay on the floor in the exact spot where he toppled. He hadn't moved a muscle, all of the noise and merriment had suddenly stopped.

"Is he dead?" someone asked.

"He's too stupid to be dead!" Ma replied as she ignored him and checked the tree to make sure it hadn't been damaged. Then she reached down and grabbed him by the shirt and hoisted him to his feet. "I told you not to drink that filthy stuff," Ma scolded him.

Grandfather was in a world of his own, but he was still sporting that stupid sort of grin on his face. Ma escorted him out of the living room and into the bedroom. "Now you've ruined everyone's Christmas just like you do every year," she wailed. "Will you never learn? Why can't you be more considerate? Think of the children. What will they think?"

She laid him on the bed and stormed out of the room, slamming the door. You could hear a pin drop as we all watched in horror. "Now everyone leave him be," she would bark in her most officious voice. "He can sleep it off and I hope that he misses Santa Claus. He doesn't deserve to see him in that condition."

Everyone scattered as Ma stomped through the living room on her way to the kitchen. When Ma was on the warpath there was always a great deal of uncertainty and a healthy respect for her orders. One didn't fool around when Ma was angry. Right now Ma was angry. We would all walk pretty softly for a while and stay out of her way.

Suddenly there was a noise on the porch and the sound of bells, and just as suddenly Ma's anger was forgotten. Grandfather was forgotten. The door flew open and with a hearty "Ho-ho-ho-Merry Christmas, Merry Christmas," Santa Claus burst through the door with a bag of toys slung on his back. He headed into the kitchen, strode past the table and on into the living room.

Straight to the Christmas tree he pranced. He set the bag of toys by the chair and then settled himself in Grandfather's chair. "Ho-ho-ho-Merry Christmas, Merry Christmas," he laughed out again. "Ho-ho-ho, have you all been good little boys and girls this year?" he asked.

"I've been a good boy, Santa." "I've been a good girl, Santa," every one of us responded, nodding our heads up and down.

Then Santa began to call each of us. "Bobby," he would call out. "Ho-ho-ho-Merry Christmas Bobby and have you been a good little boy?"

"I've been a good boy, Santa, I've been a good boy," I assured him.

"Come over here, boy, and sit on my knee. Now tell me, what did you want for Christmas this year?"

Hustling over to Santa, I climbed up on his knee. "I've been a good boy, Santa," I said. "I've been a good boy." I wanted a dump truck in the worst way, but I only ever got one present at Christmas and it was from Santa. There was no way I was going to blow it by thinking about anything else.

"Ho-ho-ho. I understand you want a dump truck, boy. Is that right?"

"I've been a good boy, Santa," I said real loud to make sure he heard me.

"Ho-ho-ho. My Elves tell me you made a bunch of roads in the dirt pile by your outhouse, boy. Now if you had a dump truck you could make more roads and use that truck to haul the dirt away."

"I've been a good boy, Santa," I pleaded with him.

"Have you, boy?" said Santa. "Have you been a real good little boy?"

"I've been a good boy, Santa."

"Ho-ho-ho," Santa laughed out as he looked in that big red bag he had sitting beside him.

WOW! My eyes about popped right out of my head when he pulled out a green dump truck. Just what I wanted. "I've been a good boy, Santa," I blurted out again as he handed me the dump truck. I climbed down off his knee and didn't see or hear another thing that was happening.

"Ho-ho-ho, Gwennie, come over here, girl, and sit on Santa's knee."

But I was lost. I was in a world of my own with my dump truck. I didn't hear anything else that was said. I didn't see anymore presents handed out. I was driving my dump truck around between chairs and legs.

Suddenly Santa was on his feet, his bag was empty and everyone was admiring the toy that Santa had brought them. "Ho-ho-ho," he laughed as he headed for the door. "Merry Christmas to all, Merry Christmas to all."

As suddenly as Santa came, he was gone. The house was very quiet again, but not because we were avoiding Ma. Ma was forgotten. Grandfather was forgotten. Santa Claus had been there. All was right with the world and we were all too busy with our individual toy. I marvelled at how Santa knew exactly what each of us had wanted and how he remembered to bring it to us.

Suddenly there was another noise, this time at the bedroom door. Grandfather had woken up and was coming back into the living room. He took his seat, the one that Santa had just left, near the tree. He still looked pretty happy and he checked to see where Ma was. She had followed Santa to the kitchen and had not come back into the living room. Grandfather winked, pulled out his Mickey and had another snort.

"You missed Santa again," I said to him. "He was just here, you missed him."

"Oh no, boy, tell me I didn't miss him again," he said with a big grin.

"You missed him again, Grandfather. He's already left."

"Did he leave me a present?" Grandfather asked reaching for his back pocket.

"He certainly did not," answered Ma. "And he won't as long as you continue to drink that filthy stuff."

Grandfather just about snapped his arm off yanking it back in front of him when he heard Ma's voice. Boy, she just about caught him that time, I thought.

Grandfather sat on his chair near the tree looking totally at ease with the world as he watched everyone playing with their gifts. That silly grin of his had spread from ear to ear. Ma looked at him and smiled, then turned and left the room. Grandfather winked and once again reached for his hip pocket.

"ME?" I ASKED

RATATAT RATATATAT I could hear the roll of the drums as I marched forward. My bugle was tucked under my right arm. My left arm was swinging shoulder-high with each step. Listening to the beat of the drums, I picked up my cue, swung the bugle up, placed it to my lips and waited, ready for the exact moment to accompany the drums. Taa ta tatata ta taa. Taa ta tata ta taa. I had memorized that sound.

At the precise moment, I puckered up and blew. Pheowwww. The air hissed through the metal tubing. There was no other sound blaring forth.

"There's something wrong with this stupid bugle," I thought as I marched along. Oh yeah, now I remember. "Purse your lips," the bugle instructor had advised. "You must get your lips tight together and squeeze the air out of them."

I pursed my lips and blew again. BLAT, BLEEEEE came the first sounds.

I had recently joined the Army Cadets and that meant I was the latest inductee into the Drum and Bugle Band.

Mom had been so excited when I came home and told her the good news that I was going to be marching in the July 1st Parade. "Right up Main Street, all the way from the CN Station to the Baseball Park," I proclaimed.

At the last meeting, I had been given my uniform and my choice of an instrument. I took the bugle, but only because there were only bugles left to take. Now I was following the instructor's direction. "You must practise every day if you want to learn to play properly."

It was Saturday morning. I had finished my chores and rushed into the house, put on my brand new uniform, polished the bugle and marched out to the driveway. Here I would march and play the bugle, out to the road where the only gate of its kind on the south road had stood, then turn smartly and march back to the house.

I knew what the roll of the drums sounded like and exactly when the bugles were to come in. As I practised my marching I was imagining the Ratatatat of the drums and at the appropriate time would swing my bugle up and join in.

My sister had come out to watch and was sitting on the rail fence beside the house. So far I had been doing a lot of marching and recalling the drums, but very little bugle playing. I was having a little trouble getting any sound to come out the end. I was beginning to think that maybe it had got stuck in there. But I persisted and my sister proceeded to drift off. That is until I finally remembered to purse my lips. I was right beside her when the first blat blew out the end of that bugle. She was so surprised, she almost fell off the fence. I was elated. I had mastered the bugle.

Down the road, Nick the Dog Man's dogs erupted in a course of howling and wailing. "Stupid dogs," I thought as I marched back and forth.

By the time the next practice rolled around, I had pretty

well conquered the bugle. I was making the sweetest music this side of heaven. This sentiment was not shared by anyone else in the family and certainly not by Nick's dogs.

I couldn't wait to show off my stuff as I strutted into the hall. Over in one corner, the drummers had gathered themselves together and were practising. There were four Majorettes in their short skirts. Two of them were twirling their batons and throwing them in the air; the other two were very busy standing around and looking so darned pretty. The largest group were the buglers. They were scattered around the rest of the hall creating all sorts of weird sounds as they warmed up.

Finally the instructor lined us all up. It was time to practice as a group. "This year, we will be leading the parade up main street on the first of July," he announced. "So we must practise, practise, practise."

I quickly grabbed a place in the front of the rows of buglers. The Majorettes would lead, followed by the drummers, then the buglers. I was right behind the drummers when we marched around the hall the first time.

This was just a practice run and only the drummers got to play. They beat time for the rest of us to march to. Around the hall I marched. I kept a close eye on the Majorettes as they strutted along lifting their knees way up. They looked like they were prancing. They sure were pretty to watch, not like some of the buglers I had the misfortune to be marching beside. It wasn't bad enough that they couldn't march near as well as I could. They kept running into me, especially on the corners.

"Troop Halt," yelled the instructor after one turn around the hall. "We have to make a few adjustments," he said and sounded totally frustrated. "This is an army platoon. You're in the army now. You are not walking down the streets like a bunch of hicks. You have to march. You pick up the step from the drums. Drummer, give me a beat please."

The drum rolled Ratat...ratat...ratat.

"Do you all hear that," shouted the instructor. "Each time the drummer plays, your left foot should be hitting the ground. Hear now, listen." As the drummer played, the instructor picked up the beat and with a singing voice, he shouted out. "LEFT...LEFT...LEFT RIGHT LEFT. Now does everyone know what to do?" he asked. "Are there any questions?"

I wanted to ask him to move the two clods on either side of me, because they kept bumping me.

Then he proceeded to move some of us around. I was disappointed to have to leave the front row and my good view of the Majorettes. But being in the third row wasn't that bad, at least I was away from the two who couldn't walk straight.

Once more we marched around the hall to the beat of the drums. I was still able to get a pretty good look at the Majorettes, especially on the corners. Just my luck though, the two goofs who were marching on either side of me now couldn't march any better then the first two. Every time I tried to get a better look at the girls, one of them would bump into me. I almost lost my bugle a couple of times.

"Troop halt," barked the instructor. "That's not much better," he snarled. "What's the matter with you people tonight? Have you forgotten how to walk in a straight line? I've never in my whole life seen so many people stumbling and falling over each other. You remind me of a bunch of ducks waddling down the ruddy road. Let's try it one more time, and if you don't do any better, we're going home. I'm not going to waste any more of my time."

He walked around the troop and looked us all over. Then he pointed at me and motioned me to come to the front of the troop.

"Me?" I asked. He probably wanted me to march out front to show them how it's done, I thought, smiling to myself. I marched past the clods that had kept bumping into me and came to a snappy halt right in front of him.

"Follow me, Mr. Adams." He smiled, then turned and walked to the rear of the troop.

I marched right along behind him, my bugle tucked neatly under my arm.

"Mr. Adams," he snarled, "I want you to march right here." Then he pointed to a spot about two paces behind the rest of the troop.

I looked around. "Right here?" I asked.

"Right here, Mr. Adams. Do I make myself clear?"

"Yes sir," I replied and looked around again. "But sir, there's no one else in my row, and I'm behind the troop!"

"That's right, Mr. Adams, and that's where you're going to stay until you learn how to march properly without running into everybody. Do you understand that, or do you want me to spell it out for you?"

"But sir," I protested, "It was those other guys. They kept bumping into me."

"We'll see," he barked. "Troop, quick march."

This time the instructor marched right along beside me. I watched the troop real carefully. Sure, I thought, this time when they knew the instructor was behind them, they marched straight. I couldn't see the Majorettes at all from way back here.

"Troop halt," yelled the instructor. "Okay, that's better now. We've only got a few more practices before the parade. I would like to try to run through the whole drill tonight if we can. Is everybody ready?" Everybody was ready. I was ready. "Troop quick march," he ordered, and we started around the hall once more.

The drummers started with their ratatatat. Then the high-stepping Majorettes twirled their batons and threw them into the air, high into the air, almost to the ceiling. Man, was this exciting, and I was a part of it. I was so pumped, I was finding it hard to concentrate. The drums were banging, I could see batons flying up in the air, I was marching and straining to hear, listening for the cue to join in with the bugle.

Then I heard it, the quick roll of the drums, RRRRRR, it was the key, notifying the buglers it was time for them to join in. Just as I had practised, I nimbly slipped the bugle from under my arm and in one fluid motion raised it to my lips. BLUEEEY it screeched out over the roll of the drums.

The guy marching right ahead of me ducked like someone had taken a shot at him. I noticed something go skittering across the floor that looked suspiciously like a baton. It crashed into the chairs lined up along the wall. Not a very good start for some, I thought.

"HALT! HALT!" I heard and noticed that none of the other buglers had raised their instruments. They had all missed the cue. The instructor was screaming as he charged to the back of the troop. His face was beet red. He stopped beside me and just stared. He was shaking so hard he could hardly speak, then he finally blurted out. "Pray tell Mr. Adams, what in the hell was that?"

"That was my bugle, Sir. I thought it was my cue to join in."

"Well Mr. Adams, you thought wrong, didn't you?"

"I guess so, Sir," I replied rather meekly. "But I'll do better next time."

"No, Mr. Adams, until you learn to play that thing, there won't be a next time. I want you to sit on the sidelines and watch for a while. Just so that you can see and hear how it's done. Then maybe, and right now that's a big maybe, I might let you try again."

"But I want to be in the first of July parade," I whined.

"We'll see, Mr. Adams, we'll see," he said. "Now if you don't mind, I would very much appreciate it if you would take a seat on the sidelines."

Dejectedly I walked over to the side and sat down. I spent the better part of that evening and many more warming up a chair as the rest of the troop marched and played.

Finally the day of the parade arrived and like the rest of the troop, I showed up at the appointed time, even though I had been told I wasn't quite ready. The instructor could hardly believe his eyes when I strutted into the staging area, in my uniform and carrying my bugle.

"What do you think you're doing here?" he asked.

"I'm going to march in the parade with my troop," I declared, looking him straight in the eye.

"I see," he answered and smiled. "And just who told you you could march in this parade?"

"My Mom did," I smiled back at him. "She's standing right over there just in case there's a problem," I informed him.

His head snapped around and he looked over at Mom. He waved and smiled at her, then turned back to me. He wasn't smiling when he said, "You'll have to march at the back of the troop, like you did at the practices. When the rest of the buglers raise their bugles, that's when you'll raise yours, and not before. Do you understand that?"

"Yes Sir," I replied with a big smile. "I can do that real good."

"I can only hope and pray," he muttered half to himself. "And one more thing, Mr. Adams, I don't want you to blow that damn bugle of yours. You put it to your lips, but you don't blow in it. Understand?"

"But Sir, I've been practising real hard. I can play it now, honest."

"Mr. Adams, I'm going to be marching right alongside of you, and if I hear one little toot coming out of your bugle, I'm going to wrap my swagger stick over your head. You get what I mean, don't you?"

"Yes Sir," I replied. "But I can play now."

"Forget it," he snapped.

I marched the length of the parade route. I listened to the ratatatat of the drums and taa ta tata ta taa of the bugles. I watched the Majorettes throw their batons into the air. I saw lots of folks that I knew. I saw Mom, as she walked along the parade route, following the troop all the way from the CN Station to the Baseball Park. I strutted and I waved to everyone.

I don't know who was the prouder, me or Mom. I have to think it was Mom though, because she told anyone who would listen that I had marched in the July 1st parade and I was the only one in the troop that was in step.

THIS IS A TURKEY SHOOT, SON

"You say your father's not here, son?" asked the man at the registration desk.

"No Sir," I replied. "He ain't here."

"Is he coming down later then?"

"No Sir. He's not at home this week."

"Well son, that's just too bad then, cause I can't do nothing for you."

"But I won the turkey," I pleaded. "I had the best score."

"That's life, son. Next time you better make sure that you shoot with your own age group."

"I can't. I used my last quarter on the last event. I don't have any money left." I was ready to cry.

"You better move along now. I've got another shoot to get underway," he said and pushed me to one side.

I had just been introduced to what it meant to be a boy competing in a man's world. There was a turkey shoot in progress on the last farm on the south road and I was one of the youngest participants.

As soon as I had finished my chores in the morning, I

had taken the remodelled .22 calibre rifle and walked the mile-and-a-half to the farm. From the top of the hill overlooking the farm, I could see the McLeod River winding along the lower field, the site of the shoot.

A number of cars and people had already arrived and were milling around. I could see the various targets. The closest ones were for the .22s and I headed straight for that area.

Some of my friends from town were already there. Most of them would be just watching, as they didn't have guns yet.

"Guess what?" said my friend Billy who had seen me coming and had run up the hill to meet me.

"What?" I asked, walking for the registration desk.

"They're gonna let Pete shoot in the kid's competition."

"How come? He's too old. He said he's 18 now. He's supposed to shoot with the men. He was bragging at school that he was going to shoot with the men this year. That's not fair."

"His Dad talked to the guy registering everybody and he agreed to let him shoot with the kids again."

"I'll never win then," I moaned.

Pete had a brand new .22 with peep sights on it and was one of the best shots in army cadets. His dad took him shooting all the time. He was about five years older than me and he always won the kids' shoots.

"It just isn't fair. Just because his Dad's a big shot in town," I complained to Billy.

I walked over to the registration desk. "I'd like to register for the kid's shoot," I said.

"You'll have to wait until we call for it," replied the registrar. "Should be in about a half-hour, son. Come back then, okay?"

"Is Pete going to shoot with the kids again this year?" I asked, praying that Billy had been wrong.

"He sure is, son. Think you can beat him?"

My heart sank at the words. "Sure, I can take him. Grandfather got his gun all fixed up for me. It's shooting real straight now."

Although Pete was one of the best shots that I knew, I felt that there was a chance that I might just beat him. In addition to Grandfather's nice sleek straight-shooting .22, I too had joined the army cadets. The firearms instructor had been a sniper in World War II and had taught me an awful lot about shooting. I no longer just threw lead at a target, I was now a very deliberate shooter. "Accuracy and grouping." The instructor had hammered home that point. "Grouping is everything." Yeah, with a little luck, I thought, I could take Pete.

"That's good," he smiled. "I bet Pete's worried sick."

It felt like they would never call for the kid's shoot. There was nothing to do while waiting except to stand around and watch the men shoot. Each time a winner was announced there would be laughing and joking. How I wanted to have my name announced.

Billy had been standing with me for a while, but then had moved over by Pete. Pete had a real following. There were a half-a-dozen kids at any one time talking to him and admiring his new rifle. Nobody came around and asked to see my rifle. I waited alone.

Finally we were called to register. There were ten shooters. I paid my 25¢ and took my place on the firing line, waiting for the range master to call us forward.

Billy walked up to me smiling. "Don't worry about Pete," he said. "He won't hit nothing today, you'll take him easily." He winked like he knew something that I didn't.

"Yeah, sure," I replied. "How do you know?"

"Okay boys," called the range master. "Let's move up to the line now."

We all walked forward and laid down on a mat. I cast a quick glance at Pete. For a guy who won't hit anything today, he sure looked confident. I looked back at Billy and he was grinning from ear to ear.

"You boys each know which target you're shooting at?" the range master asked.

Everybody indicated that they did and commenced shooting. The slim .22 felt wonderful in my hands and I proceeded to fire my 10 shots at my target. Everything felt real good; I knew I had a good target. All my shots must have been in the black because I couldn't see a single mark on the white of the target. I looked over at Pete's target and sighed. He didn't have a single shot showing in the white, either.

We all walked down to retrieve our targets. I looked at mine and my spirits rose. I had a perfect score. Pete couldn't beat me, only tie. I grabbed my target and ran over to where Pete was standing, looking in disbelief at his target. It was still hanging, as pure as the driven snow. There wasn't a mark on it. Pete had missed every shot.

Everyone was gathering around. "What happened, Pete?" someone asked him. "Shoot at the wrong target?"

"I don't know," he mumbled. "I was sure I was shooting at mine. Anyone have extra bullet holes in the centre of their target?" he asked, looking around.

I looked at my target again and counted the bullet holes. Ten. Suddenly I had a sickening thought. Maybe Pete had shot my target and I had shot at someone else's. Somewhere there had to be a target with too many holes in it.

The range master collected all the targets including

Pete's and went over to the registration desk to confer with the registrar.

"Bob Adams, can you come over to the registrar's desk, please," I heard someone yell.

My first thought was that they had found my bullets in someone else's target. My friend Billy walked over with me.

"Congratulations, son. You won yourself a turkey," the registrar said. He handed me a slip of paper. "You take this into Jack's Meat Market and he'll give you a nice big one." He smiled at me and stuck out his big hand. I took the paper and shook hands with him. I was shaking like a leaf.

"I won, Billy!" I said, hardly able to believe it. "I won a turkey."

"I told you you'd win," he laughed.

"How'd you know?" I asked.

"That stupid Pete was letting everybody look at his rifle and he gave it to some guys to hold. I saw them screwing up the peep sight." Billy was laughing so hard he could hardly stand up. "I figured he'd be lucky to hit the far end of the field the way everybody was playing with them sights. Man, you should have seen the look on his face when he walked down there and seen his target."

"I'm going to go and see if I can shoot again," I said, full of confidence now that I had already won.

I walked back over to the registrar and asked if there was another kid's shoot.

"Sure is son, but you've already won one turkey, I don't know if that's fair," he replied. "I think maybe we should give someone else a chance to win."

"Well, you let Pete shoot with us kids, and that wasn't fair," I replied.

"Tell you what son, you go get your Daddy and have him come talk to me first. Okay?"

"My Dad's not here."

"He's not!" He acted surprised. "Well that's too bad son, but I think we'll give one of the other boys a chance to win a turkey." He gave me a big fatherly smile.

"But that's not fair," I protested. "Just because I won doesn't mean that I can't shoot again."

"Tell you what, son. If you really want to shoot again, I have an idea. You're a pretty good shot, you know," he said convincingly. "How'd you like to try your luck against the men?"

"How much does it cost to shoot with the men?" I asked.

"One dollar, son. Just one dollar."

"I don't have a dollar."

"Well, how much you got, son?" He was being real polite.

"I got two bits is all," I replied.

"I'll tell you what I'm going to do for you, son. I'm going to let you shoot with the men for the price of a kid, just 25¢. Now, how does that sound?"

"I guess so," I replied. I wasn't too sure that I wanted to shoot with the men.

"Don't do it," Billy whispered to me. "He just wants to take your quarter."

"What do you say, son? A boy who shoots as good as you do ought to be able to shoot with the men. Are you man enough to try?"

That was a challenge I couldn't pass up. I gave him my quarter and took my place on the line.

There were lots of comments and laughter from the men as I stood there waiting to start. "Hey," one of the shooters yelled at the range master, "you make sure that kid knows which target he's supposed to shoot at. This next turkey's got my name on it and I don't want an extra hole in my target." More laughter that was hard to ignore.

"Hey kid," someone yelled at me. "You want to give me a couple of your shells? I'll put them in the bull's-eye for you. Show you what a good shot looks like."

"That gun looks awful big for a little guy like you. Want me to hold it for you, boy?" another chipped in. They sure didn't like me competing with them.

I was relieved when the range master gave us instructions to commence. The comments stopped when the shooting started.

When the shooting was finished, I went down and looked at my target. I puffed out my chest; I had shot another perfect score. These guys might tie me, I smiled, but none of them are going to beat me.

"Looks like you won yourself another turkey," said the range master as he took my target. "No one else got a target that looks this good."

"What the hell do you mean, he won another turkey?" one of the other shooters shouted. "That bloody kid shouldn't be shooting with the men. There's kids' shoots here, that's where he belongs."

That started a lot of yelling and shouting between the registrar and some of the other shooters. I didn't really care, I just wanted my slip to get another turkey, then I'd leave. I didn't have any more money anyway, but I had two turkeys. Would Mom ever be surprised, I thought.

When the shouting and yelling stopped, I went over to the registrar and asked for my slip.

"Sorry son," he looked at me without smiling. "You shouldn't have shot with the men. Kids are supposed to shoot with the kids. I've already given the turkey to the man with the best score in the last group."

"But I had the best score," I wailed. "I beat all of those guys."

"Well, I guess you should have stayed with the kids then, shouldn't you?"

"I wanted to, but you wouldn't let me. You made me shoot with the men."

"That's your tough luck, son. You better run along now."

"Can I get my quarter back so's I can shoot with the kids next time?" I pleaded.

"Sorry. This is a turkey shoot, son. I just take money in, I don't give it out. Now you run along like a good kid. I got more events to run."

"Yeah, well you would if my Dad was here," I said with tears in my eyes.

"I told you," Billy said. "He just wanted your quarter."

I SMELL LIKE COWSHIT

"Bobby," Mom called at an ungodly hour of the morning. "It's time to get up now."

I looked up and she was standing in the doorway. As soon as she left, I rolled over and went back to sleep.

"Up you get now, come on, get moving." Mom was back, this time by the side of the bed. "The cows have to be milked and the chickens fed before you go to school. Now hurry, or you'll be late. Ted won't wait for you if you're late."

Ted Sliva had a dairy farm south of our farm, and every morning he delivered milk into Edson. He also picked up all of the kids on the south road and gave them a ride to school. He was the unofficial school bus. His only pay was a thank you.

"I'll have breakfast ready when you're finished," Mom called out.

With those words I started another day. Winter had set in on the south road. Dad had left yesterday to work in the bush camps for the winter and the daily task of milking the cows and feeding the chickens was now my responsibility.

There were times when it was not an advantage to be the oldest child. Early morning chores was certainly one of those times.

Whenever Dad was away, Mom would pump me up pretty good. "You're the man of the house," she would say and I would strut around acting like 'the man of the house.' Then, as things needed doing, she would mention all the chores that came with the title, 'the man of the house.'

The first chore was milking the cows. It needed to be done twice a day and the early morning milking was the worst. As I swung my legs over the side of the bed, I suddenly realized the title, 'the man of the house,' didn't seem near as glamorous as it did yesterday.

"Man, is it ever dark," I thought, as I dragged my butt out of bed in the middle of the night. The only light in the house was from the kerosene lantern that Mom had lit earlier. It was hanging from a nail over the table in the kitchen and it cast a few rays through the open bedroom door.

I groped for my socks and unable to find them, accidentally put my feet on the floor. I was instantly jarred into reality by the shock of my nice warm feet on the ice cold linoleum. It sent a chill throughout my body. What a kick-start to get you moving real fast. It didn't matter how long I would stand on one spot, the lino never got any warmer. My feet just got colder and colder. It was not a time for one to dally.

Once dressed, I lit a gas lantern and walked outside. "Man, is it ever cold," I mumbled, as I headed for the barn to milk the cows. Thank heaven the barn was always nice and warm even in the coldest weather.

I set the lantern on the floor right behind the cow I was going to milk first. "You hang that lantern on the hook in the ceiling," I remembered Dad saying when I had tried this stunt earlier. "If that cow kicks you could burn the whole barn down and everything in it." I picked it up and hung it properly on the ceiling where its light would show on each cow that was to be milked.

Each cow was given a pitch fork of hay to munch on while being milked. This offering was usually enough to keep them satisfied while I gathered the stool and pail and settled in beside the first old girl to commence milking. Sitting on the stool with my feet under the cow's belly, I would begin to rhythmically pull the teats, first one then the other. The milk made a rhythmic sound as it swished into the pail.

We had several cats in the barn and they loved to get fresh milk. There was a dish sitting over by the wall and the cats were eager to have their morning milk. One of them was rubbing up against my leg and purring. Cats have a pretty easy life, I was thinking to myself, as I pointed a teat in the direction of the dish and aimed a stream of milk at it. Dad didn't approve of this either, I thought. I missed the dish and was busily lining up another shot.

Suddenly, I found myself laying on the floor against the wall at the back of the barn. What the heck happened here, I thought, as I looked around and tried to gather my senses.

The milk pail that had been held tightly between my legs as I stroked the teats was lying on the floor on the other side of the cow. Milk had splashed all over the barn floor and was being lapped up by the cats. The milk stool was lying behind the cow, right where the lantern had been. Good thing I moved it, I thought. I was covered in hay, straw and cow shit.

As I lay there, it dawned on me. The bloody cow had kicked me. It was a good thing I didn't have a bad temper.

I got up and walked over to the pail and picked it up. It was empty, I had lost all the milk. Boy was I going to get it from Mom.

"Stupid cow," I muttered, and took a swift kick at her. This prompted her to return the favour. She just about connected again. I jumped to the side to avoid the flying hoof, lost my balance and fell to the floor again. That did it. I'd had enough of being 'the man of the house.'

"That miserable cow kicked me," I said as I stormed through the door carrying the lantern and the empty pail. "I'm never going to milk her again."

"Didn't you put on the kickers?" Mom asked.

"No, I forgot."

"Bobby, Bobby, Bobby," Mom moaned. "If you've been told once, you've been told a hundred times to put those kickers on. Why can't you ever do what you're told?"

"Well, I'm never going to milk that stupid cow again. I hope she gets milk fever and dies. Just look at me," I wailed. "I'm covered with cow shit and I smell like cow shit. I can't go to school like this. I need some clean clothes."

"I see you didn't manage to save any of the milk," she said, looking at the empty pail, ignoring my plight.

"No, I didn't," I snapped back.

"Did you finish milking the cow?"

"No I didn't and I said I'm not going to milk that stupid cow anymore."

"What about the other cows? Did you milk them?"

"No," I replied, suddenly remembering that there was more than one cow in the barn.

"Then you get right back out there and finish your chores and this time you'd be wise to put on the kickers. That's what they're there for. You had better hurry or you'll be walking to school this morning. Your ride won't

197

wait for you."

"Is breakfast ready?" I asked, hoping to postpone the inevitable.

"Yes it is," Mom replied. "Just as soon as you've finished your chores."

Reluctantly I picked up the lantern and the milk pail and headed back to the barn.

"Get over you miserable old cow," I yelled as I walked up beside the stall and looked at the cow. She was eyeballing me right back. We stared at each other for a couple of minutes and then I went and grabbed the kickers. "I'll fix her," I chuckled to myself.

By now the cows had finished the hay I had given them earlier. My friend the kicker was watching. She was not having anything to do with me entering her stall again. As I approached the stall with the kickers in my hand, she let fly with another hind foot. She was quick, but I was quicker and her hoof whizzed by harmlessly. I got around to the side of the stall and tried to reach through and get one of the kickers onto her far leg. This time I wasn't nearly fast enough. She sent the kickers flying and me sprawling into the other stall.

Man, now I was really getting mad. I was mad at that stupid cow for not letting me into the stall; I was mad at Mom for making me go back to the barn. I had a problem. For some strange reason, on this morning, I wanted to go to school, but both Mom and the stupid cow stood in my way.

I knew I had to finish milking before I went back to the house. Maybe if I was nice to her, I thought. I talked real slow, low and gentle like. I even patted her on the side and on the rump all the time, talking real slow. I even tried to sing a couple of cowboy songs as I tried to sneak the kickers on.

Whap, another kick. Both the kickers and myself flew in different directions. Now I was furious.

I tried everything I could think of, but each time I got close to that stupid cow, she would kick out. But I persisted and I think that cow finally just got plain tired of kicking. Suddenly as I reached around the side of the stall, she just stood there and I slipped a kicker on one leg and then zip on the other.

I grabbed the milk pail and the stool and once again sat myself down at the side of the cow. At last I could finish my chores. This time I wasn't nearly as gentle with her and every time she moved, I would slug her with my fist. I was not about to forgive that miserable beast. Besides being mad and bruised, I had a constant reminder of her earlier victory. I couldn't shake the smell of cow shit.

When I finished the milking, I grabbed the lantern and the milk pail and left the barn. It seemed to be awfully light. I didn't need the lantern anymore and turned it off. Usually it was still dark when I finished all my chores.

I stopped at the chicken coop to throw out a handful of wheat for the chickens and check to see if there were any eggs. When I entered the coop, I dared those chickens to do one stupid thing and if they did I knew for sure we would have chicken for supper that night. The chickens were smarter than the stupid cow. I fed them and collected the eggs. Then I was off to the house for a change of clothes and some breakfast.

"We need some water, before you take your clothes off," Mom informed me as I walked through the door. "You be careful that you don't get any of that manure in the well or the pail or you'll be going right back and getting some more. Now get a move on."

"I wanna change first," I said.

"You can change when you're finished. Now get a move on, you're already late."

I grabbed the water pail, kicked the door open and stormed out of the house. This just wasn't my day, I thought. At the well I lifted the lid and tossed the pail down the shaft. This had to be done just right so that the pail landed on its side and would fill with water. If it was dropped straight down it would land on its bottom and float. I knew I could do this right. The pail quickly filled with water and I hoisted it out of the well, hand over hand. I filled the water pail and headed for the house.

I kicked my boots off and put the water on the stand. I glared at Mom, just daring her to call me 'the man of the house' and hit me with another job.

"Don't take your clothes off just yet," she said. "While you're dressed, you might as well bring some wood in and fill the wood box," Mom directed.

There, she did it. Just to spite me. I hadn't suffered enough, now I had to fill the wood box, too. "Why can't someone else do that? I have to do everything around here," I mumbled. "I'm hungry and I have to hurry or I'll be late and Ted won't wait for me. You just want me to miss my ride," I said accusingly.

"There's no one else here. Ted's already picked them up, they've all left for school. Now hurry up and fill the wood box. Your breakfast is getting cold."

"Sure, I do all the work and what thanks do I get for it? Cold breakfast. Cold oatmeal," I grumbled as I walked back out the door.

There wasn't enough wood split, so I had to do that in order to fill the wood box. I grumbled all the time and cursed that stupid cow. If she hadn't kicked over the milk pail none of this would have happened.

When I finished the chores, I changed my clothes and washed up as best I could. But I couldn't get rid of the smell of cow shit. It was like it was ground right into my skin.

"I'm not going to school today," I informed Mom. I decided to exercise some of the privileges of being 'the man of the house.'

"You eat your breakfast and then you can march yourself right into town, young man. I'll not hear any more talk about not going to school."

"But Mom," I howled. "I smell like cow shit. I can't go to school smelling like this. Everybody will laugh at me."

"I'll melt some snow today and you can have a bath when you come home tonight. Now hurry up, you're already late."

"They won't let me into the school if I'm late," I argued.

"Oh yes they will," Mom replied. She was always a step ahead of me. "I've already written a note for your teacher telling her that you had a little run-in with the cow this morning. She'll understand."

"You won't have to tell her about the cow. She'll be able to smell me, everybody will. Please Mom, don't make me go." I was reduced to begging.

I walked to school by myself. I cursed that stupid cow every step of the way. I cursed Mom. I smelled of cow shit. I sat in school for the rest of the day with this unique odour emanating from my body.

Previously my classmates had learned that I came from a 'stump farm'. That day several of them told me that they never really knew what a 'stump farm' was, but now they knew what one smelled like.

GIVE *"THE STUMP FARM"* TO A FRIEND

MEGAMY PUBLISHING LTD.

BOX 3507

SPRUCE GROVE, ALBERTA, CANADA T7X 3A7

Send to:

Name_____

Street_____

City_____

Province/   Postal/
State_____Code/Zip_____

Please send_____copies of *"The Stump Farm"*

Enclosed is $14.95 + $4.00 for Postage and Handling plus 7% GST
per book.($20.27 ea.) Total amount enclosed $_____

Make cheque or money order payable to

"MEGAMY PUBLISHING LTD."

✂-------U.S. orders payable in U.S. funds.-------------------------

GIVE *"THE STUMP FARM"* TO A FRIEND

MEGAMY PUBLISHING LTD.

BOX 3507

SPRUCE GROVE, ALBERTA, CANADA T7X 3A7

Send to:

Name_____

Street_____

City_____

Province/   Postal/
State_____Code/Zip_____

Please send_____copies of *"The Stump Farm"*

Enclosed is $14.95 + $4.00 for Postage and Handling plus 7% GST
per book.($20.27 EA.) Total amount enclosed $_____

Make cheque or money order payable to

"MEGAMY PUBLISHING LTD."

U.S. orders payable in U.S. funds.

GIVE *"THE STUMP FARM"* TO A FRIEND

MEGAMY PUBLISHING LTD.

BOX 3507

SPRUCE GROVE, ALBERTA, CANADA T7X 3A7

Send to:

Name_____

Street_____

City_____

Province/   Postal/
State_____Code/Zip_____

Please send_____**copies of** *"The Stump Farm"*

Enclosed is $14.95 + $4.00 for Postage and Handling plus 7% GST
per book.($20.27 ea.) Total amount enclosed $_____

Make cheque or money order payable to

"MEGAMY PUBLISHING LTD."

✂------------------------U.S. orders payable in U.S. funds.--------------------------

GIVE *"THE STUMP FARM"* TO A FRIEND

MEGAMY PUBLISHING LTD.

BOX 3507

SPRUCE GROVE, ALBERTA, CANADA T7X 3A7

Send to:

Name_____

Street_____

City_____

Province/   Postal/
State_____Code/Zip_____

Please send_____**copies of** *"The Stump Farm"*

Enclosed is $14.95 + $4.00 for Postage and Handling plus 7% GST
per book.($20.27 EA.) Total amount enclosed $_____

Make cheque or money order payable to

"MEGAMY PUBLISHING LTD."

U.S. orders payable in U.S. funds.

GIVE *"THE STUMP FARM"* TO A FRIEND

MEGAMY PUBLISHING LTD.

BOX 3507

SPRUCE GROVE, ALBERTA, CANADA T7X 3A7

Send to:

Name_____

Street_____

City_____

Province/   Postal/
State_____Code/Zip_____

Please send_____**copies of** *"The Stump Farm"*

  Enclosed is $14.95 + $4.00 for Postage and Handling plus 7% GST
  per book.($20.27 ea.) Total amount enclosed $_____

Make cheque or money order payable to

"MEGAMY PUBLISHING LTD."

✂-----------------U.S. orders payable in U.S. funds.----------------------------

---

GIVE *"THE STUMP FARM"* TO A FRIEND

MEGAMY PUBLISHING LTD.

BOX 3507

SPRUCE GROVE, ALBERTA, CANADA T7X 3A7

Send to:

Name_____

Street_____

City_____

Province/   Postal/
State_____Code/Zip_____

Please send_____**copies of** *"The Stump Farm"*

  Enclosed is $14.95 + $4.00 for Postage and Handling plus 7% GST
  per book.($20.27 EA.) Total amount enclosed $_____

Make cheque or money order payable to

"MEGAMY PUBLISHING LTD."

U.S. orders payable in U.S. funds.